First World War

and Army of Occupation

War Diary

France, Belgium and Germany

42 DIVISION
Divisional Troops
Royal Army Medical Corps
1/2 East Lancashire Field Ambulance
6 March 1917 - 28 February 1919

WO95/2652/2

The Naval & Military Press Ltd
www.nmarchive.com
Published in association with The National Archives

Published by

The Naval & Military Press Ltd

Unit 10 Ridgewood Industrial Park,

Uckfield, East Sussex,

TN22 5QE England

Tel: +44 (0) 1825 749494

www.naval-military-press.com

www.nmarchive.com

Contents

Document type	Place/Title	Date From	Date To
Heading	WO95/2652/2 42 Divn. 1/2 E Lancs Field AMB 1917 Mar-1919 Feb		
Heading	42nd Division 1-2nd East Lancs FLD Ambulance Mar 1917-1919 Feb		
Heading	War Diary 1/2 East Lancashire Field Ambce Vol III From March 6th to March 31. 1917		
War Diary	Marseilles On Board H.M.T. Huntspill	06/03/1917	06/03/1917
War Diary	Enroute	06/03/1917	08/03/1917
War Diary	Huppy	09/03/1917	29/03/1917
War Diary	Fontaine Sur Somme	30/03/1917	31/03/1917
War Diary	War Diary. 1/2 East Lanc. Field Ambce. April-30. 1917 Vol. IV 1917		
War Diary	Fontaine Sur Somme	01/04/1917	06/04/1917
War Diary	Chuignolles	07/04/1917	23/04/1917
War Diary	Marly Camp Chuignolles.	24/04/1917	30/04/1917
Diagram etc	Improvised Vapour And Sulphur Bath.		
Heading	War Diary Of 1/2 East Lancashire Field Ambulance. From 1st May To 31st May 1917 Medical Services. Volume V		
War Diary	Marly Camp. Chuignolles	01/05/1917	04/05/1917
War Diary	Peronne	04/05/1917	08/05/1917
War Diary	Templeux La. Fosse	09/05/1917	16/05/1917
War Diary	62 C J 4 a Central	17/05/1917	17/05/1917
War Diary	Bertincourt	17/05/1917	20/05/1917
War Diary	Royaulcourt	21/05/1917	31/05/1917
Miscellaneous	Royal Army Medical Corps 42nd Division Order No. 8. App I	05/05/1917	05/05/1917
Operation(al) Order(s)	Operation Order No. 1 by Major A. Callam Cmdg. 1/2nd. E. Lancs. Field Ambulance. App 2	05/05/1917	05/05/1917
Diagram etc	App 3		
Miscellaneous	A Form. Messages And Signals. App 4		
Operation(al) Order(s)	Operation Order No 1A by Major Callam Cmdg 1/2nd E L Fd Amb.	14/05/1917	14/05/1917
Operation(al) Order(s)	Addendum To Royal Army Medical Corps 42nd Division Order No. 9 App 6	19/05/1917	19/05/1917
Operation(al) Order(s)	Royal Army Medical Corps 42nd Division Order No. 9	15/05/1917	15/05/1917
Operation(al) Order(s)	Reference R.A.M.C., 42nd Division Order No. 9 of 15th inst.	18/05/1917	18/05/1917
Miscellaneous	To/O.C., 1/2nd Fld Ambulance	15/05/1917	15/05/1917
Miscellaneous	To/O.C., 1/2nd East Lancs Fld Ambce	15/05/1917	15/05/1917
Operation(al) Order(s)	127th Infantry Brigade Order No. 15	16/05/1917	16/05/1917
Operation(al) Order(s)	March Table. To accompany 127th Infantry Brigade Order No. 15	16/05/1917	16/05/1917
Miscellaneous	Ammendment To 127th Infantry Brigade Order No. 16	16/05/1917	16/05/1917
Miscellaneous	O.C., 1/2nd E.L. Field Ambulance.	16/05/1917	16/05/1917
Miscellaneous	Move Of 42nd Division. Continuation Of Administrative Instructions.	16/05/1917	16/05/1917
Miscellaneous	O.C. 1/2nd Ex Fld Amb.	16/05/1917	16/05/1917
Miscellaneous	To O.C. 1/2nd Field Amb.	16/05/1917	16/05/1917

Operation(al) Order(s)	Royal Army Medical Corps 42nd Division Order No. 10	16/05/1917	16/05/1917
Operation(al) Order(s)	Field Ambulance Operation Orders No. 2. by Major. A. Callam R.A.M.C.T. A/O.C. 1/2nd. East Lancashire Field Ambulance. App 10		
Diagram etc	Sick Wounded Admitted M.D.S. 1/2 L.F.A.		
Miscellaneous			
Diagram etc	Brigade Sick		
Miscellaneous	App 12		
Diagram etc	Scabies Cases Treated at M.D.S 1/2 E L F. Amb.		
Miscellaneous	App 13		
Heading	War Diary Of 1/2 East Lanc. Field Ambce. 42nd Division. Vol. VI 1-30 June 1917		
War Diary	Ruyaulcourt	01/06/1917	30/06/1917
Map	Appendix 4		
Operation(al) Order(s)	Operation Orders No 3 by Lt. Col W.R. Mathews R.A.M.C.T. O.C. 1/2nd. East Lancashire Field Ambulance.	04/06/1917	04/06/1917
Operation(al) Order(s)	Operation Orders No 4 by Lt. Col. W.R. Matthews R.A.M.C.T. O.C. 1/2nd East Lancashire Field Ambulance. Appendix 3		
Miscellaneous	Gas Poisoning. General Lines Of Treatment Adopted. Appendix 4	30/06/1917	30/06/1917
Heading	War Diary Of 1/2nd East Lancashire Field Ambulance. From July 1st, 1917 To July 31st, 1917. (Volume VII)		
War Diary	Ruyaulcourt.	01/07/1917	04/07/1917
War Diary	Ruyaulcourt 67 C. P 10 C. 4.4	05/07/1917	05/07/1917
War Diary	Gomiecourt. 57 C. A23 C 8.2	06/07/1917	31/07/1917
War Diary	Gomiecourt	31/07/1917	31/07/1917
Operation(al) Order(s)	1/2nd. East Lancashire Field Ambulance Order No. 5. By Lt. Col. W.R. Matthews. R.A.M.C.T. Appendix 1	05/07/1917	05/07/1917
Miscellaneous	Scheme of Training Appendix II.		
Miscellaneous	Daily Rate of Sick During the Month of July 1917. Appendix 3	00/07/1917	00/07/1917
Miscellaneous	Sick Wounded Chart July 1917	00/07/1917	00/07/1917
Miscellaneous			
Miscellaneous	Summary of Seabie Patients Treated Month ending July 31st/17	31/07/1917	31/07/1917
Miscellaneous	Scabies Chart for July 1917	00/07/1917	00/07/1917
Miscellaneous			
Heading	War Diary Of 1/2nd (East Lancashire Field Ambulance. From 1st August, 1917. To 31st August, 1917. (Volume VIII)		
War Diary	Gomiecourt. 57 C A 23 C 8.2	01/08/1917	18/08/1917
War Diary	Gomiecourt	19/08/1917	19/08/1917
War Diary	Bouzincourt.	20/08/1917	22/08/1917
War Diary	274 19b 8.6	23/08/1917	25/08/1917
War Diary	Red Farm 28 G5d 9.5	26/08/1917	31/08/1917
Miscellaneous	Orders by Lieut.-Colonel. W.R. Matthews. R.A.M.C. T.F. O.C. 1/2nd. E. Lancs. Field Ambulance. Appendix I	19/08/1917	19/08/1917
Miscellaneous	Orders by Lieut.-Colone W.R. Matthews. R.A.M.C.T.F. O.C. 1/2nd. E. Lancs. Field Ambulance. Appendix II	22/08/1917	22/08/1917

Miscellaneous	Orders by Lieut,-Colonel. W.R. Matthews. R.A.M.C.T.F. O.C. 1/2nd. E. Lancs. Field Ambulance. Appendix III	24/08/1917	24/08/1917
Miscellaneous	Orders by Lieut.-Colonel. W.R. Matthews. R.A.M.C.T.F. O.C. 1/2nd. E. Lancs. Field Ambulance. Appendix IV	30/08/1917	30/08/1917
Diagram etc Miscellaneous	Sick August 1917 Appendix V		
Heading	War Diary of O.C., 1/2nd East Lancs. Field Ambulance. From 1st September 1917 to 30th September 1917 (Volume IX)		
War Diary	Red Farm 28 G 5d 95	06/09/1917	18/09/1917
War Diary	Winnezele Area	19/09/1917	20/09/1917
War Diary	Wormhudt. Area	21/09/1917	21/09/1917
War Diary	Teteghem	22/09/1917	22/09/1917
War Diary	Lapanne	23/09/1917	24/09/1917
War Diary	Oost Dunkerke Bains	25/09/1917	30/09/1917
Operation(al) Order(s)	Movement Order No. 6 By Lt. Col. W.R. Matthews. R.A.M.C.T.F. O.C. 1/2nd. East Lancashire Field Ambulance. Appendix 1	18/09/1917	18/09/1917
Miscellaneous	Reveille 5. moved off in morning to new ground at other side of Winnezeele.	20/09/1917	20/09/1917
Operation(al) Order(s)	Movement Order No 7. By Lt. Col. W.R. Matthews. R.A.M.C.T.F. O.C. 1/2nd. East Lancashire Field Ambulance. Appendix 2	20/09/1917	20/09/1917
Operation(al) Order(s)	Movement Order No 8. By Lt. Col. W.R. Matthews. R.A.M.C.T.F. O.C. 1/2nd. East Lancashire Field Ambulance. Appendix 3	21/09/1917	21/09/1917
Operation(al) Order(s)	Movement Order No 9. By Lt. Col. W.R. Matthews. R.A.M.C.T.F. O.C. 1/2nd. East Lancashire Field Ambulance. Appendix 4	22/09/1917	22/09/1917
Miscellaneous			
Operation(al) Order(s)	Movement Order No. 10 By Lt. Col. W.R. Matthews. R.A.M.C.T.F. O.C. 1/2nd. East Lancashire Field Ambulance. Appendix 5	24/09/1917	24/09/1917
Diagram etc Miscellaneous	Sick September 1917		
Heading	War Diary of O.C., 1/2nd East Lancashire Field Ambulance. 1st October 1917 to 31st October 1917. Volume 10		
War Diary	Oostdunkerke Bains.	01/10/1917	06/10/1917
War Diary	X 13.6.50	07/10/1917	31/10/1917
Operation(al) Order(s)	Movement Order No 11. By Capt. W.J. Purves. R.A.M.C.T.F. For O.C. 1/2nd. East Lancashire Field Ambulance. Appendix I	04/10/1917	04/10/1917
Operation(al) Order(s)	Movement Order No 12. By Lt. Col. W.R. Matthews. R.A.M.C.T.F. O.C. 1/2nd. East Lancashire Field Ambulance. App II	28/10/1917	28/10/1917
Diagram etc Miscellaneous	Sick October 1917. Appendix III		
Diagram etc Miscellaneous	Sick Wounded Treated Of A.D.S. Appendix IV		
Heading	War Diary Of 1/2nd East Lancashire Field Ambulance. From-1st November, 1917 To 30th November, 1917. (Volume XI)		
War Diary	X 7 C 8.7	01/11/1917	18/11/1917

War Diary	Wormhudt	19/11/1917	21/11/1917
War Diary	Co Ehm	22/11/1917	27/11/1917
War Diary	Merville	28/11/1917	30/11/1917
Operation(al) Order(s)	1/2nd. East Lancashire Field Ambulance Order No. 12 App I	15/11/1917	15/11/1917
Operation(al) Order(s)	1/2nd. East Lancashire Field Ambulance Order No 13 App II	17/11/1917	17/11/1917
Operation(al) Order(s)	1/2nd. East Lancashire Field Ambulance Order No 14 App III	25/11/1917	25/11/1917
Heading	War Diary Of 1/2nd East Lancashire Field Ambulance. From December 1st, 1917 To December 31st, 1917 Volume XII		
War Diary	Merville	01/12/1917	04/12/1917
War Diary	Bethune College des Jeun Nesaules	05/12/1917	05/12/1917
War Diary	College dis Jeunnes Filles Bethune	06/12/1917	25/12/1917
War Diary	College des Jeunnes Filles	26/12/1917	27/12/1917
War Diary	Locon X 13.b.9.5	28/12/1917	31/12/1917
Operation(al) Order(s)	1/2nd. East Lancashire Field Ambulance Order No 14 By Lt. Col. W.R. Matthews. R.A.M.C.T.F.	12/12/1917	12/12/1917
Heading	War Diary Of 1/2nd East Lancashire Field Ambulance. From January 1st, 1918 To January 31st, 1918 (Volume I)		
War Diary	Locon X 13 b.9.5	01/01/1918	11/01/1918
War Diary	Mesplaux Farm	11/01/1918	31/01/1918
Heading	War Diary Of 1/2nd East Lancashire Field Ambulance. From February 1st, 1918 To February 28th, 1918. (Volume 2)		
War Diary	Mesplaux Farm Nr. Locon	01/02/1918	12/02/1918
War Diary	Cantrainne	13/02/1918	28/02/1918
Heading	War Diary Of 1/2nd East Lancashire Field Ambulance, R.A.M.C. (T.F.) From. March 1st, 1918 To March 31st, 1918. (Volume III)		
War Diary	Cantrainne	01/03/1918	23/03/1918
War Diary	Ayette	24/03/1918	26/03/1918
War Diary	Lacauchie	26/03/1918	29/03/1918
War Diary	Gaudiempre	30/03/1918	31/03/1918
Heading	War Diary Of 1/2nd East Lancashire Field Ambulance From April 1st, 1918 To April 30th, 1918. (Volume IV)		
War Diary	Guadiempre Souastre	01/04/1918	08/04/1918
War Diary	Marieux	09/04/1918	16/04/1918
War Diary	Bayencourt	17/04/1918	27/04/1918
War Diary	Souastre	28/04/1918	30/04/1918
Heading	War Diary Of 1/2nd East Lancashire Field Ambulance. From. May 1st, 1918. To May 31st, 1918. (Volume V)		
War Diary	Souastre	01/05/1918	05/05/1918
War Diary	Henu	06/05/1918	31/05/1918
Heading	War Diary Of 1/2nd East Lancashire Field Ambulance. From June 1st, 1918 To June 30th, 1918. (Volume VI)		
War Diary	Henu	01/06/1918	06/06/1918
War Diary	Bus in Artois	07/06/1918	27/06/1918
War Diary	Bus	28/06/1918	30/06/1918
Heading	War Diary of 1/2nd East Lancashire Field Ambulance. From July 1st, 1918. To July 31st, 1918. (Volume VII)		
War Diary	Bus	01/07/1918	04/07/1918
War Diary	M.D.S. Bus.	05/07/1918	28/07/1918
War Diary	Bus. Les Artois.	29/07/1918	31/07/1918

Heading	War Diary Of 1/2nd East Lancashire Field Ambulance. From 1st August 1918 to 31st August 1918 Volume VIII.		
War Diary	M.D.S. Bus.	01/08/1918	24/08/1918
War Diary	Cowrcelles au-Bois	25/08/1918	25/08/1918
War Diary	Miraumont	26/08/1918	29/08/1918
War Diary	Pys	30/08/1918	31/08/1918
Heading	War Diary Of 1/2nd East Lancashire Field Ambulance. September 1st 1918 to September 30th 1918. Volume IX.		
War Diary	Pys	01/09/1918	02/09/1918
War Diary	M 12a 39	03/09/1918	03/09/1918
War Diary	N 18 b 5. 8	04/09/1918	05/09/1918
War Diary	M 12.a. 3.9	06/09/1918	20/09/1918
War Diary	Ruyaulcourt	21/09/1918	30/09/1918
Heading	War Diary Of 1/2nd East Lancashire Field Ambulance. October 1st 1918 to October 31st 1918. Volume X.		
War Diary	Royaulcourt	01/10/1918	07/10/1918
War Diary	Ribecourt	08/10/1918	08/10/1918
War Diary	Lesdain	09/10/1918	09/10/1918
War Diary	Esnes	10/10/1918	10/10/1918
War Diary	Beauvdis	11/10/1918	19/10/1918
War Diary	Prayelle	20/10/1918	20/10/1918
War Diary	Veesley	21/10/1918	23/10/1918
War Diary	Beauvdis	24/10/1918	31/10/1918
Heading	War Diary Of 1/2nd East Lancashire Field Ambulance From November 1st, 1918 To November 30th, 1918. (Volume XI)		
War Diary	Beauvdis I 16Q14 57 B 1/4000	01/11/1918	03/11/1918
War Diary	Solesmes	04/11/1918	04/11/1918
War Diary	Beaudigni	05/11/1918	05/11/1918
War Diary	Le Quesnoy	06/11/1918	08/11/1918
War Diary	Maison Rouge	09/11/1918	10/11/1918
War Diary	Hautmont	11/11/1918	30/11/1918
Heading	War Diary of 1/2nd East Lancashire Field Ambulance From December 1st 1918 To December 31st 1918. (Volume XII)		
War Diary	Hautmont	01/12/1918	12/12/1918
War Diary	Grand Reng (Belgium)	14/12/1918	14/12/1918
War Diary	Binche (Belgium)	15/12/1918	15/12/1918
War Diary	Fontaine Leveque	16/12/1918	17/12/1918
War Diary	Montignies Sur-Sambre	18/12/1918	31/12/1918
Heading	War Diary Of 1/2nd East Lancashire Field Ambulance From January 1st, 1919 To January 31st, 1919. (Volume 1)		
War Diary	Montignies Sur Sambre	01/01/1919	31/01/1919
Heading	War Diary. 1/2nd East Lancashire Field Ambulance. Vol. II February 1-28th 1919		
War Diary	Montignies Sur Sambre	01/02/1919	28/02/1919

WO 95 2652/2

42 DIVN. 1/2 E LANCS FIELD AMB

1917 MAR – 1919 FEB

42ND DIVISION

1-2ND EAST LANCS FLD AMBULANCE

MAR 1917 - ~~DEC 1918~~ 1919 FEB.

Confidential

Vol 2

140/2042

WAR DIARY

1/2 EAST LANCASHIRE FIELD AMBCE

VOL. III.

FROM MARCH 6th TO MARCH 31.
1917.

Army Form C. 2118

Instructions regarding War Diaries and Intelligence Summaries are contained in F. S. Regs., Part II. and the Staff Manual respectively. Title Pages will be prepared in manuscript.

WAR DIARY
or
~~INTELLIGENCE SUMMARY~~
(Erase heading not required.)

Place	Date 1917 MARCH	Hour	Summary of Events and Information	Remarks and references to Appendices
MARSEILLES.	6.	9. AM.	Reached MARSEILLES at daybreak this morning: waiting for M.L.O. and E.M.O.	
ON BOARD HMT HUNTSPILL		10 AM.	Handed over tick to E.M.O; handed over keys of drugstore + panniers to CHIEF STEWARD of ship + received receipt. W.R.M.	
		11 AM	DISEMBarking stores + equipment; train due to leave at 2 p.m. for destination; means for getting stores out of hold very deficient: fear will not get all stores off ship before train time; have arranged for baggage party to remain behind if necessary to see to Equipment; rations for journey to be drawn at station. W.R.M.	
EN ROUTE		3 p.m.	On board train: all officers + men on train; under protest have had to leave rest of baggage behind in charge of infantry guard: fear that there will be losses on the way; complained to C.O. train but no satisfaction; accommodation on train very bad; no windows to carriages + no lavatory facilities; anticipate cold journey W.R.M.	
		9 pm.	On the way; railway arrangements very bad. W.R.M.	
EN ROUTE.	7.	9 pm.	Cold journey: arrangements for feeding bad. W.R.M.	
EN ROUTE	8.	9 pm.	Weather still cold and snow lying all round: arrangements for getting hot water for men + food for officers very deplorable W.R.M.	

Instructions regarding War Diaries and Intelligence Summaries are contained in F. S. Regs., Part II. and the Staff Manual respectively. Title Pages will be prepared in manuscript.

WAR DIARY
or
INTELLIGENCE SUMMARY
(Erase heading not required.)

Army Form C. 2118

Place	Date 1917 MARCH	Hour	Summary of Events and Information	Remarks and references to Appendices
HUPPY	9.	9pm.	Reached PONT REMY at 11 pm. and detrained equipment stores and personnel; waggons motor with baggage sent on in front with one officer and billetting party to take over billets; rest of personnel and A.S.C. attached by route march to village of HUPPY some 12 KILOS distant; reached HUPPY at 5 a.m. men marched well and no casualties on the way; officers and men in billets: hospital in farm steading. W.R.M.	REF. MAP ABBEVILLE 14 FRANCE 1/100000
	10.	9pm.	Opened hospital in FARM STEADING: two wards and dressing room with small room for officers ward; personnel in the farm buildings above hospital and round yard; rest of men in barn attached to Chateau some 200 yds distant; N.C.O.S. billetted in CAFE: officers chargers under cover in good stabling: drew and took on charge TRANSPORT consisting of 20 H.D., 17 L.D., 2 riders with emergency harness; also took on charge 3 AMB. WAGGONS H.D., 6 G.S. P.D., 4 Double limbers, 3 WATERCARTS, 1 MALTESE CART; 9 sets of double harness not P.D. G.S., 7 double sets of P.D. G.S., 1 single set S.D.: took also on charge but not yet arrived 7 AMB. WAGGONS MOTOR consisting 5 DAIMLER 2 FORD and 2 MOTOR CYCLES TRIUMPH; billetted in 126 BDE AREA and receiving sick of 1/4 EAST LANC REGT and 1/10 MANCH. REGT, rest of BDE not arrived; also receiving sick of M.G.C. of 126 BDE + details of 126 BDE H.Q: evacuating to 2 STATIONARY HOSPITAL, ABBEVILLE. W.R.M.	

1875 Wt. W593/826 1,000,000 4/15 J.B.C. & A. A.D.S.S./Forms/C. 2118.

Instructions regarding War Diaries and Intelligence Summaries are contained in F. S. Regs., Part II. and the Staff Manual respectively. Title Pages will be prepared in manuscript.

WAR DIARY

or

INTELLIGENCE SUMMARY

(Erase heading not required.)

Army Form C. 2118

Place	Date 1917 MARCH	Hour	Summary of Events and Information	Remarks and references to Appendices
HUPPY.	11.	9pm.	MOTOR AMBULANCES and Drivers reported for Duty also 2 MOTORCYCLES. All the equipment of the cars except a few details which have been reported are complete: the cars are in good condition + evidently not been much used; sick are being evacuated twice daily to ABBEVILLE at 10 A.M. and at 2 p.m.; the number of sick from the units not great and there seems to be no prevailing disease except those associated with catarrhal conditions; there are still cases of SCABIES reporting from the units in the BDE.; sections of the Field AMBULANCE are doing duty in turn at the RECEP-TION HOSPITAL; fire DRILLS arranged for; water carts filled & tested daily for the condition of the water; horses of the TRANSPORT are out in the open in a road form-ing a cul-de-sac; standings are bad after the wet but no other available. W.R.M.	REF. MAP. ABBEVILLE 14 FRANCE 1/100,000
	12.	9pm.	Remainder of baggage and equipment and stores drawn today; some things missing which has been reported to A.D.M.S. in a letter not accepting responsibility for any losses incurred by the refusal to allow baggage party to remain behind; carrying on the routine of Hospital duties and refitting + equipping the unit. W.R.M.	
	13.	9pm.	Nothing special to note; weather bad + cold; sick keeping moderate. W.R.M	
	14	9pm.	Nothing special to note; work carrying on: superintending the bathing arrange-ments for the BDE. find that can do easily 50 men an hour. W.R.M.	

1875 Wt. W593/826 1,000,000 4/15 J.B.C. & A. A.D.S.S./Forms/C. 2118.

Instructions regarding War Diaries and Intelligence Summaries are contained in F. S. Regs., Part II. and the Staff Manual respectively. Title Pages will be prepared in manuscript.

WAR DIARY
or
~~INTELLIGENCE SUMMARY~~

(Erase heading not required.)

Army Form C. 2118

Place	Date 1917 MARCH	Hour	Summary of Events and Information	Remarks and references to Appendices
HUPPY	15	9pm.	Nothing special to note; men doing hospital duties and route marches and TRANSPORT employes in route march every other day & the intervening day in harness cleaning: the harness received in a very bad state and will require lots of work on it to get it right; seems to have been neglected: suitable but not serviceable for work of TRANSPORT. W.R.M.	REF. MAP. ABBEVILLE 14 FRANCE 1/100,000
	16.	9pm.	Reported the condition & unsuitableness of harness to A.D.M.S.; efforts to be made to replace it: difficulty in getting numeral branding irons. W.R.M.	
	17.	9pm.	Nothing special to note; CAPTAIN TURNER & 1 NCO. detailed for attachment for duty with the 1st Division by authority of A.D.M.S.; they report for duty tomorrow at A.D.M.S. Office & travel by motor to destination. W.R.M.	
	18	9pm.	Captain TURNER & 1 NCo left for duty with 1st Division; 1 NCo. & 3 O.R. left for ten days leave to ENGLAND; orders received that MAJOR GEORGE ASHTON to take command of 2/2 EAST LANC. FD. AMB. 66th Division vice MAJOR A. CALLAM who is to report for duty with this unit. W.R.M.	
	19.	9pm.	Nothing special to note; hospital routine, route marches & bathing duties being carried out satisfactorily: weather still very cold. W.R.M.	
	20.	9pm.	Nothing special to note; average admissions to hospital keeping low; no prevailing disease: some cases of scabies and Catarrh and Tonsillitis. W.R.M.	

1875 Wt. W593/826 1,000,000 4/15 J.B.C. & A. A.D.S.S./Forms/C. 2118.

Instructions regarding War Diaries and Intelligence Summaries are contained in F. S. Regs., Part II. and the Staff Manual respectively. Title Pages will be prepared in manuscript.

WAR DIARY

or

INTELLIGENCE SUMMARY

(Erase heading not required.)

Army Form C. 2118

Place	Date 1917 MARCH	Hour	Summary of Events and Information	Remarks and references to Appendices
HUPPY	21.	9pm.	Nothing special to note; carrying out Hospital & section routine: very little sickness in the unit in spite of the climatic conditions W.R.M.	REF MAP ABBEVILLE. 14. FRANCE 1/100000
	22.	9pm.	Nothing special to note: men & horses well; drawing for horses very bad. W.R.M.	
	23	9pm.	Received orders to draw 4 Riders from A.S.C. Advanced Depot ABBEVILLE: 2 riders to be held in charge for 1/1st Field AMBulance. W.R.M.	
	24	9pm.	Took on charge 4 Riders today: nothing special to note; weather cold. W.R.M.	
	25.	9pm.	Nothing special to note; allotted bath about 500 men per diem. W.R.M.	
	26	9pm.	Changed 9 double sets of harness for P.D.G.S. today: nothing else to note. W.R.M.	
	27.	9pm.	Saw A.D.M.S. reference remarks by A.A.&Q.M.G. on TRANSPort report & took reception to it in reply. W.R.M.	
	28.	9pm.	Issued out box respirators and gas helmets today and had a lecture by GAS OFFICER in the morning and fitting of respirators; in gas chamber where lachrymatory gas used this afternoon men entered & tested their respirators. All the men tested except those only of TRANSPORT: they being done tomorrow: received orders to move with 126 BDE to LIERCOURT on 30th. W.R.M.	

1875 Wt. W593/826 1,000,000 4/15 J.B.C. & A. A.D.S.S./Forms/C. 2118.

Army Form C. 2118

Instructions regarding War Diaries and Intelligence Summaries are contained in F. S. Regs., Part II. and the Staff Manual respectively. Title Pages will be prepared in manuscript.

WAR DIARY
~~or~~ ~~INTELLIGENCE SUMMARY~~
(Erase heading not required.)

Place	Date 1917 MARCH	Hour	Summary of Events and Information	Remarks and references to Appendices
HUPPY	29.	9pm.	Issued orders for move to FONTAINE on the 30th by route march; part of baggage + equipment moved today; billets arranged for the unit by billeting party; orders for 2 NCOs or men to go on leave: detailed 1 NCO + 1 OR. W.R.M.	REF. MAP. ABBEVILLE 14 FRANCE. 1/100000.
FONTAINE sur SOMME	30	9pm.	Field Ambulance left HUPPY by Route march in column of sections at 1.30 pm; orders for 5 minutes halts at the half hours and ten minutes halt at the clock hour on the march; men marched well and reached FONTAINE at 5 pm.; no casualties on the way; men in good billets: hospital in the school buildings; 1 NCO + 1 OR left on leave: MAJOR G. ASHTON reported from leave to England	
	31	-	Had inspection of billets; men comfortable and NCO + officers billetted near; latrine arrangements are difficult; water arrangements too are not safe; [illegible] factory; sanitation bad; orders for men not to drink any water but from the carts + also enjoined not to eat food or beverages from cafés that has not been cooked; sick not high from units; a few cases of diarrhoea in unit but otherwise health of unit good; no bad feet after the route march; 2 OR left on 10 days leave today; weather during the month has been cold + wet + conducive to catarrhs & tonsillitis. W.R.M.	

W. R. Matthews
Lt Col RAMC T.F.
O.C. 1/2 East Lancs. Fd. Ambce
42nd Divn.

1875 Wt. W593/826 1,000,000 4/15 J.B.C. & A. A.D.S.S./Forms/C. 2118.

Vol 3

42nd Div
140/2086

WAR DIARY.

1/2 EAST LANC. FIELD AMBCE.

APRIL 1 - 30. 1917.

VOL. IV. 1917.

April 1917

Instructions regarding War Diaries and Intelligence Summaries are contained in F. S. Regs., Part II. and the Staff Manual respectively. Title Pages will be prepared in manuscript.

WAR DIARY
or
INTELLIGENCE SUMMARY
(Erase heading not required.)

Army Form C. 2118

Place	Date 1917 April	Hour	Summary of Events and Information	Remarks and references to Appendices
FONTAINE SUR SOMME	1	9pm.	Saw A.D.M.S. reference the working of Divisional Baths at HALLENCOURT; inspected with the acting C.R.E. the proposed arrangements; await instructions as to when to take over the supervision: MAJOR ASHTON left by MOTOR to take command of 2/2 East Lanc Fd. Ambce 66th Division: 2 O.R. on leave to ENGLAND. W.R.M.	REF MAP ABBEVILLE 14 FRANCE 1/100000.
	2.	9pm.	Inspected all billets; found satisfactory; horselines very bad standing; men are contented; food is good & almost full ration; received instructions to be ready to move on 6th by route march; sickness rate keeping low in spite of cold weather & the wet: one or two cases of diarrhoea which are due to some irritation arising from some ingesta taken: no evidence of anything else. W.R.M.	
	3.	9pm.	Drew pay for men today; had a visit from BRIGADIER 126th BDE reference move on 6th and the dealing with UNFIT to march; made certain suggestions which he approves of: horse casualty; 3 H.D. short; A section practised loading waggons today: loaded ready to move in half an hour. W.R.M.	
	4.	9pm.	Drew two days rations today in anticipation of move; received telegram to attend at BDE. HQRS to receive orders about move; indented for extra motor waggon for surplus stores and rations; wired A.D.M.S for authority to get three H.D. horses to fill up casualties. W.R.M.	
	5.	9pm.	Unit moving by rail on the 7th inst; TRANSPORT moving by route march to new area; orders received + instructions given to transport; CAPTAIN A. GIBSON detailed to go in charge of transport; CAPTAIN TURNER + 1 OR leaving as advanced party on the 6th by	

1875 Wt. W593/826 1,000,000 4/15 J.B.C. & A. A.D.S.S./Forms/C. 2118.

Instructions regarding War Diaries and Intelligence Summaries are contained in F. S. Regs., Part II. and the Staff Manual respectively. Title Pages will be prepared in manuscript.

WAR DIARY
or
~~INTELLIGENCE SUMMARY~~

(Erase heading not required.)

Army Form C. 2118

Place	Date 1917 April	Hour	Summary of Events and Information	Remarks and references to Appendices
FONTAINE SUR SOMME	5	9pm.	motor lorry; received instructions from A.D.M.S to takeover dressing station at CHUIGNOLLES; took on charge 3 H.D. W.R.M.	REF MAP. ABBEVILLE 14
	6	9pm.	TRANSPORT less AMBULANCE WAGGONS left this morning en route by route march for CHUIGNOLLES under CAPTAIN GIBSON; CAPTAIN TURNER and 1 O.R. left with advance party for CHUIGNOLLES; rest of baggage moved to PONTREMY to move by rail; FIELD AMBULANCE less 1 NCO + ten men moving by train tomorrow from PONTREMY at 8 A.M.; convoy of motor cars moving by road to CHUIGNOLLES; hospital to be closed at 10 AM. tomorrow; all patients being evacuated to ABBEVILLE. W.R.M.	FRANCE 1/100000
CHUIGNOLLES.	7.	9pm.	Reached CHUIGNOLLES this afternoon by route march from LA FLAQUE Railhead; taken over 4 hutments in MARLEY CAMP next to Divisional Rest STATION; two hutments for personnel and two for hospital purposes; reported arrival to A.D.M.S; taken over patients from 1/3 EAST LANC. FD. AMBULANCE; evacuating sick from 126 BDE and Div. Hd. Qrs.; men stood the march well + marched well in spite of extra load on pack. W.R.M.	REF MAP AMIENS 17 FRANCE 1/100000 REF. MAP 1/40000
	8	9pm.	TRANSPORT with baggage and equipment under CAPTAIN GIBSON reported arrived by lorry; no casualties amongst horses or men; horses stood the test well; Rest of baggage not yet arrived by train. MAJOR H.W. PRITCHARD + W.R.M. CAPTAIN WEBSTER detailed for duty with 39 C.C.S. III Corps orders.	62D R4 C52.

1875 Wt. W593/826 1,000,000 4/15 J.B.C. & A. A.D.S.S./Forms/C. 2118.

Army Form C. 2118

Instructions regarding War Diaries and Intelligence Summaries are contained in F. S. Regs., Part II. and the Staff Manual respectively. Title Pages will be prepared in manuscript.

WAR DIARY
or
INTELLIGENCE SUMMARY

(Erase heading not required.)

Place	Date 1917 APRIL	Hour	Summary of Events and Information	Remarks and references to Appendices
CHUIGNOLLES	9	9pm.	TWO HOSPITAL wards running with patients from 126 BDE + Div. H.Q; most of the patients are suffering from conditions resulting from the cold weather; a certain amount of scabies two reporting; condition of ground round camp deplorable. Health & spirit is good in spite of cold weather. W.R.M.	REF. MAP AMIENS 17 FRANCE 1/100000.
	10	10pm.	MAJOR A. CALLAM from 2/2 EAST LANC FIELD AMBulance reported to-day for duty with the unit; orders received that 126 BDE moving to new area; gave instructions for two horse AMBULANCE WAGGONS to follow in rear of the 126 BDE + to be at place appointed by 10.A.M. W.R.M.	
	11	10pm.	126 BDE moved to new area to-day: BDE H.Qrs at FRISE; 1/4 EAST LANC at ECLUSIER; 1/5 EAST LANC. at ECLUSIER; 1/9 MANCHESTER at FEULLIERS; 1/10 MANCHESTER at camp on road between FLAUCOURT + HERBECOURT; AMBULANCE WAGGON picked up 10 cases who were all fit to return to units; stores have arrived that went by rail from PONTREMY in waggon. W.R.M.	REF MAP 62C FRANCE 1/40 000.
	12.	9pm	CAPTAIN GIBSON detailed for duty with the 1/8th MANCHESTER REGT: delivered 1000 AMMONIA AMPOULES to different units in BDE.; notified BDE of the number of men who fell out on march; special instructions received from D.M.S. 4th ARMY reference treatment of gas cases + fractures. W.R.M.	
	13.		DIV. H QRS moving to PERONNE on 14th inst; nothing special to note W.R.M.	

1875 Wt. W593/826 1,000,000 4/15 J.B.C. & A. A.D.S.S./Forms/C. 2118.

Instructions regarding War Diaries and Intelligence Summaries are contained in F. S. Regs., Part II. and the Staff Manual respectively. Title Pages will be prepared in manuscript.

WAR DIARY

~~or~~

~~INTELLIGENCE SUMMARY~~

(Erase heading not required.)

Army Form C. 2118

Place	Date 1917 APRIL	Hour	Summary of Events and Information	Remarks and references to Appendices
CHUIGNOL-LES.	14	9p.m.	Nothing Special to NOTE. W.R.M.	REF MAP. AMIENS 17 FRANCE 1/100000
	15	9pm.	CAPTAIN J.J. HUMMEL returned from leave to ENGLAND; 126th BDE moving forwards on the 16th + 17th inst: 1/10 MANCH. REGT to LONGAVESNES on 16th; 1/4 EAST LANC. REGT to PERONNE on 16th; detailed waggon Ambulance Horse to follow in rear of 1/4 EAST LANC REGT. W.R.M.	REF MAP. 62C. FRANCE 1/40,000
	16	10pm.	CAPTAIN HUMMEL detailed to relieve CAPTAIN GIBSON as M.O. temporarily i/c of 1/8 MANCH. REGT; detailed 2 H.D. AMB. WAGGONS to follow in rear of 126 BDE on the 17th inst to PERONNE + to be at Cross Roads HERBECOURT at 7.45 A.M. 3 MOTOR AMBCE WAGGONS detailed to report to O.C. 1/1 EAST LANC FD AMBCE by authority of A.D.M.S. W.R.M.	
	17.	10pm.	MAJOR CALLAM detailed to go to PERONNE to look at building for DRESSING STATION. Detailed working party of 1 NCO + 18 men to go to PERONNE; received instructions for A.D.M.S. to form DRESSING STATION at PERONNE on the 18th; detailed MAJOR CALLAM + CAPTAIN TURNER and one section and one bearer subdivision to go by route march tomorrow the 18th to PERONNE; sick from DIVISION EAST of PERONNE to be evacuated by this unit + collected by the 1/1st S.M. F.A. until Dressing station ready. W.R.M.	REF MAP ~~[illegible]~~ 62C I 27 C 4.4

Instructions regarding War Diaries and Intelligence Summaries are contained in F. S. Regs., Part II. and the Staff Manual respectively. Title Pages will be prepared in manuscript.

WAR DIARY
or
~~INTELLIGENCE~~ SUMMARY
(Erase heading not required.)

Army Form C. 2118

Place	Date 1917 APRIL	Hour	Summary of Events and Information	Remarks and references to Appendices
CHUIGNOL-LES.	18	11pm.	MAJOR CALLAM, CAPTAIN TURNER with one section and one bearer subdivision went by route march to PERONNE today reached destination without any casualties; CAPTAIN G.B. JAMESON reported for duty from the 1/5 EAST LANC REGT. A DRESSING STATION to be formed at PERONNE. W.R.M.	REF MAP. 62C. FRANCE 1/40,000
	19.	9pm.	CAPTAIN GIBSON + 40 O.R. went on leave today for ten days to ENGLAND; MAJOR CALLAM reported that DRESSING STATION ready to receive patients; three motor AMBULANCES attached to DRESSING STATION for duty; evacuating sick from 42nd Division EAST of PERONNE. W.R.M.	REF MAP AMIENS 17 FRANCE. 1/100,000
	20	9pm.	NOTHING special to report; 32 cases admitted to Hospital today. W.R.M.	
	21.	9pm.	VISITED DRESSING STATION at PERONNE today and found everything satisfactory + in an advanced state of preparedness under MAJOR CALLAM. W.R.M.	
	22.	11pm.	Received orders from A.D.M.S. that this unit will form the DIVISIONAL REST STATION when room available; preparations in anticipation made. W.R.M. 235 PATIENTS passed through Hospital during week 14–21 April 1917.	
	23.	9pm.	Visited A.D.S. at PERONNE and found everything in a forward state for the receiving + treatment of casualties and of certain sick; wards ready for the reception of wounded; D.R.S. station at MARLY CAMP being carried out as far as it is possible with the accommodation provided at present and until the 1st DIVISIONAL REST CAMP moves from its present site. W.R.M.	

1875 Wt. W593/826 1,000,000 4/15 J.B.C. & A. A.D.S.S./Forms/C. 2118.

Instructions regarding War Diaries and Intelligence Summaries are contained in F. S. Regs., Part II. and the Staff Manual respectively. Title Pages will be prepared in manuscript.

WAR DIARY ~~or~~ ~~INTELLIGENCE~~ SUMMARY

(Erase heading not required.)

Army Form C. 2118

Place	Date 1917 April	Hour	Summary of Events and Information	Remarks and references to Appendices
MARLY CAMP CHUIGNOLLES.	24	9pm.	It is noted that most of the cases coming into D.R.S. are cases of what is called SCABIES but really PEDICULOSIS in many cases with staphylococcic infection as well: method of treating this condition by means of sulpho-steam vapour baths being carried out at A.D.S. under MAJOR CAPPOLATTA, which seems very successful. W.R.M.	REF. MAP 1/40000 62 P R 4 C 52.
	25	9pm.	Nothing special to note: health of unit very good: no sick reporting. W.R.M.	
	26	9pm.	Visited A.D.S. at PERONNE & found things satisfactory; disinfection of Scabies being carried out satisfactorily: CAPTAIN HUMMEL formerly with 1/8 MANCHESTER REGT. W.R.M.	
	27	9pm.	Ninety one patients in hospital; no prevailing disease; cases not of serious character & chiefly sores & catarrhs. W.R.M.	
	28.	9pm.	Nothing special to note: 125 patients in D.R.S.; nothing of special note. The improvement in the weather should mitigate the sickness rate. W.R.M.	
	29	9pm.	Nothing special to note: 136 patients admitted into D.R.S. last week ending 28th. 26% Scabies, 25% N.Y.D. FEVER 3% Diarrhoea. No prevailing disease. W.R.M.	
	30	9pm	Instructed O.C. 'C' Section to detail CAPTAIN TORNER + 12 O.R. to take over Dressing Station at TINCOURT-BOUCLY on 2nd MAY. Health of unit good during the month; certain number been on 10 day leave; unit 6 under strength.	REF. MAP. 62c J28 6.

W.R. Matthews
Lt Col RAMC T.
OC. 1/2 East Lancs Fd Amb

1875 Wt. W593/826 1,000,000 4/15 J.B.C. & A. A.D.S.S./Forms/C. 2118.

Improvised Vapour and Sulphur Bath.

5' 1"
5' 0"
4' 0"
2' 0"
2' 0"
Front Elevation.

Detail of Sliding Door.

3'-9"
3'-7"
1'-1"
1'-5"
1'-1"
4'-9"
4'-3"
Side Elevation

Detail of Sliding Panel (Top).

6'-1"
3'-9"
6"
Top of Cabinet.

5' 0"
Back Elevation (Reduced scale)

Steam Generator

Inside.

MEDICAL SERVICES.

CONFIDENTIAL.

— WAR —
— DIARY —

OF

1/2ND EAST LANCASHIRE FIELD AMBULANCE.

FROM 1st MAY TO 31st MAY 1917.

(VOLUME V.)

Army Form C. 2118

Instructions regarding War Diaries and Intelligence Summaries are contained in F. S. Regs., Part II. and the Staff Manual respectively. Title Pages will be prepared in manuscript.

WAR DIARY

~~or~~

~~INTELLIGENCE SUMMARY~~

(Erase heading not required.)

Place	Date 1917 MAY	Hour	Summary of Events and Information	Remarks and references to Appendices
MARLY CAMP. CHUIG-NOLLES.	1	9pm	Received 49 patients from 1/1st EAST LANC. FD. AMBCE. at CAPPY; over 200 patients in D.R.S.; quite a number of admissions with boils; drew Eight EP.I.P. (European pattern) tents and 80 Stretcher trestles, for D.R.S. re-innoculated half of the personnel with T.A.B; given instructions that the personnel at M.D.S. to be re-innoculated also. W.R.M.	REF.MAP 62.D.R 4.C52 FRANCE. 1/40,000
	2.	9pm.	Visited M.D.S. at PERONNE; found satisfactory; itch treatment proceeding in a satisfactory manner & evidently efficacious; admissions to D.R.S. chiefly NYD FEVER & Boils. W.R.M.	
	3.	9pm.	Nothing special to be noted; going on 15 days leave to ENGLAND; MAJOR CALLAM in charge of unit; MAJOR H.W. PRITCHARD in charge at CAMP MARLY of D.R.S. W.R.M.	
	4		ON LEAVE.	

Instructions regarding War Diaries and Intelligence Summaries are contained in F. S. Regs., Part II. and the Staff Manual respectively. Title Pages will be prepared in manuscript.

WAR DIARY
or
~~INTELLIGENCE SUMMARY~~

(Erase heading not required.)

Army Form C. 2118.

Place	Date	Hour	Summary of Events and Information	Remarks and references to Appendices
PERONNE	May 4th	-	Headquarters of Field Ambulance moved from CHUIGNOLLES (62D. R.4 d 4.8.) to PERONNE (62C. I 24) Major Pritchard RAMC T. left in charge of DRS at CHUIGNOLLES – Dispositions of the unit are now as follows – PERONNE – Divisional MDS. C. Section less 1 officer + 12 O.R. at TINCOURT (62C J 24 a) B. " Bearer. Subdivision. CHUIGNOLLES – DRS. A. Section B Section Tent subdivision. TINCOURT. ADS. 1 officer + 12 O.R.	
" "	" 5	-	RAMC 42nd Div. Operation order No 8. received and orders issued accordingly	App 1 / 2
" "	6	-	Bearer subdivision B. Sect. under command of Capt Gibson moved from PERONNE to TEMPLEUX-LA-FOSSE (62C. D28d.) & took over site from 1/1st E.L. Fd Amb. – move reported complete by 10 am – satisfactory.	
" "	7	-	Reference Op order 8 para 3. orders received for detachment at TINCOURT to proceed direct to TEMPLEUX LA FOSSE on the 8th inst. after handing over to 1/2nd S. MIDLAND FD AMB. Visited TEMPLEUX LA FOSSE with ADMS. 42nd Div. & selected new site for DRS at 62C. J 5a central	App 1
" "	8	-	Move to TEMPLEUX LA FOSSE as laid down in operation order No 8 completed by 6 PM. – Divisional MDS opened at 6 PM all moves satisfactorily completed. Dispositions are now as follows – Divisional MDS – A Sect. + B + C Bearer subdivisions (less 5 OR employed on Scabies treatment PERONNE) DRS. CHUIGNOLLES – B Sect. Tent Sub. PERONNE – C Sect " " + SCABIES-personnel.	App 3

2449 Wt. W14957/M90 750,000 1/16 J.B.C. & A. Forms/C.2118/12.

Instructions regarding War Diaries and Intelligence Summaries are contained in F. S. Regs., Part II. and the Staff Manual respectively. Title Pages will be prepared in manuscript.

WAR DIARY
or
~~INTELLIGENCE SUMMARY~~
(Erase heading not required.)

Army Form C. 2118.

Place	Date	Hour	Summary of Events and Information	Remarks and references to Appendices
TEMPLEUX LA FOSSE	" 9	–	ADMS 42nd DIV visited MDS & site for DRS. (62C J4 a central) – Construction of DRS commenced & improvements in MDS – material available one ADRIAN HUT. – one Hospital NISSEN Hut incomplete. 12 EPIP. New pattern marquees & 2 large tarpaulins (30 x 20) Evacuation – sick likely to be fit in 14 days DRS, not " " " " 5 + 48 CCS BRAY. Wounded – 34 + 55 CCS LA-CHAPELETTE.	App / Ht
" "	" 11	–	Reinforcement of RAMC 3 OR's arrived from Base.	Ht
" "	" 13	–	Reinforcement of ASC HT 2 OR's arrived from 42nd Divisional Train.	Ht
" "	" 14	–	Orders received from above to evacuate PERONNE DRS. All cases to be sent to DRS-CAMP MARLY. –CHUIGNOLLES. – Instructions issued accordingly. Operation order No 1 A – Personnel &c to move to TEMPLEUX LA FOSSE when completed.	App 4, 5 / Ht
" "	" 15	11-30 am	DRS. PERONNE reported evacuated – MDS. visited by DDMS III Corps & ADMS 42nd Div. – satisfactory	
	–	6.30 PM	Orders received that a 7th Amb 2nd Cavalry division would take over MDS. TEMPLEUX LA FOSSE on 16.5.17 & that the unit would move by route march in conjunction with 124th Inf Bde & concentrate in the YTRES AREA, B sect tent subdivision to remain at DRS – CAMP, MARLY. Evacuation during move while in III Corps area to Divisional MDS TEMPLEUX LA FOSSE & while in XV Corps area to 2 MDS, FINS. (57C 1/20000 V12 central)	App 6
	–	10-20 PM	Orders received from 124 Bde to send billeting party 1 Off 1 NCO. to report to DAAQMG 20th Divn (P26 b 5 ½) at 12 noon 16.5.17 & to be in readiness to move main body early morning 17.5.17.	Ht " 7
" "	16	10. am	B section tent-subdivision moved from PERONNE TO TEMPLEUX LA FOSSE. Move completed by 10 am	Ht
	–	12 noon	Divisional MDS handed over to 4th Cavalry Division – moved out & bivouacked for night on site of (new) DRS. 62C J 4 a central) – Surplus stores dumped at VILLERS FAUCON under divisional arrangements	
62C J 4 a central	17.	5-30 am	Moved out in conjunction with 124 Inf Bde, forming starting point 62C D12 c 7.2 7-10 am. in accordance with march table. route TEMPLEUX LA FOSSE – NURLU. MANANCOURT – YTRES – BERTINCOURT. Motor transport route – BUSSU, ST. DENIS – HAUT-ALLAINES. – MANANCOURT – ROCQUIGNY – YTRES – BERTINCOURT.	" 8 / Ht

2449 Wt. W14957/M90 750,000 1/16 J.B.C. & A. Forms/C.2118/12.

Instructions regarding War Diaries and Intelligence Summaries are contained in F. S. Regs., Part II. and the Staff Manual respectively. Title Pages will be prepared in manuscript.

WAR DIARY
or
INTELLIGENCE SUMMARY
(Erase heading not required.)

Army Form C. 2118.

Place	Date	Hour	Summary of Events and Information	Remarks and references to Appendices
BERTINCOURT	17	12 noon	Arrived BERTINCOURT & encamped there – 1 officer & 6 OR who fell out during the march were returned to their units – Reception station for Brigade opened. Move actually satisfactory & without a hitch. ADMS 20th Div visited camp & gave instructions for evacuation &c while under administration of 20th Div.	
"	"	4 PM	Visited ADS ROYAULCOURT at present run by the 61st Fd Ambulance & arranged to visit line on 18.5.17 to arrange relief in accordance with Divl. operation order No 10 & [illegible] orders for relief on 19.5.17. A gradual relief in the line was arranged commencing midday 18.5.17 in order that NCOs & men would become familiar with the area & routes of evacuation. All relief to be complete by 6 PM 19.5.17.	App. 9 " 10
"	" 18	12 noon	Visited the line accompanied by Capt [illegible] & an officer detailed by OC 61st Fd Amb. Divisional line runs from HAVRINCOURT WOOD inclusive through TRESCAULT to VILLERS PLOUICH. Of that line 61st Fd Amb were evacuating LEFT BRIGADE & left half of CENTRAL BDE – RAP.s are situated at following places 57C SE 1/20000 – reading from Rt – LEFT. Q14 Central – Q7 b 65 – Q1 c 40 – P6 b 99. & RAP.s for support battalions are at P18 d 92 & P18 b 27.– Evacuation from these points is carried out by means of wheeled stretchers to FD AMB. LOADING POSTS at P18 d 31 for Centre BDE & P12 b 50 for LEFT BGDE – At each of these LOADING POSTS a FORD CAR is stationed for evacuation to ADS. ROYAULCOURT. In the event of wet weather it becomes impossible to get a car up to LOADING POST P12 b 50 consequently a RESERVE LOADING POST is established at P12 a 13. & car stationed there – Personnel & accommodation at POSTS & ADS and method of evacuation are as shown in appendix 12. 1 NCO & 16 men relieved a corresponding number of men of 61st Fd Ambulance. Reinforcement ASC MT 1 OR. arrived – Capt Gibson reported to 1/5 [illegible] for temporary duty as Reg MO.	App. 11.
"	" 19		Took over whole of line evacuated by 61st FD Amb in accordance with [illegible] operation order No 10. Relief completed by 6 PM. – satisfactory.	
"	" 20.		Arrangements made to increase accommodation at ADS. for patients & personnel & working parties commenced, to undertake the work. O. Commanding returned from leave.	

2449 Wt. W14957/M90 750,000 1/16 J.B.C. & A. Forms/C.2118/12.

A Callam [illegible]

Army Form C. 2118.

Instructions regarding War Diaries and Intelligence Summaries are contained in F. S. Regs., Part II. and the Staff Manual respectively. Title Pages will be prepared in manuscript.

WAR DIARY
or
INTELLIGENCE SUMMARY

(Erase heading not required.)

Place	Date 1917 MAY	Hour	Summary of Events and Information	Remarks and references to Appendices
ROYAULCOURT.	21	9pm.	RETURNED from leave last night; found FIELD AMBULANCE forming A.D.S at village of ROYAULCOURT and Relay posts, loading posts and bearer posts near and in HAVRINCOURT WOOD. 57C P18 Q.13, 14. W.R.M.	REF MAP 57C P10 C.4.4. FRANCE 1/40,000.
	22	9pm.	Handed over to 1/1st EAST LANC FIELD AMBULANCE one loading post, MILL FARM 57C P24 B 6.2 and two bearer posts. W.R.M.	
	23	9pm.	Visited the loading posts and bearer posts and R.A.P. today and found all satisfactory. W.R.M.	
	24	9pm.	Nothing special to note. W.R.M.	
	25	9pm.	It is noted that when THOMAS HIP SPLINT is applied for extension in fracture of the femur that there is difficulty in carrying the stretcher owing to the increased length of patient + splint and thereby causing the stretcher bearers to constantly come into contact with the splint + cause pain to the patient. The Sulpho-vapour baths for Itch cases being carried out successfully. W.R.M.	
	26	9pm.	Visited relay post and altered its construction so as to be shell proof; sickness rate seems to be keeping up and mostly N.Y.D FEVER. W.R.M.	
	27.	9pm.	Nothing special to note. W.R.M.	

2449 Wt. W14957/M90 750,000 1/16 J.B.C. & A. Forms/C.2118/12.

Instructions regarding War Diaries and Intelligence Summaries are contained in F. S. Regs., Part II. and the Staff Manual respectively. Title Pages will be prepared in manuscript.

WAR DIARY
or
INTELLIGENCE SUMMARY
(Erase heading not required.)

Army Form C. 2118.

Place	Date 1917 MAY	Hour	Summary of Events and Information	Remarks and references to Appendices
ROYAUL-COURT.	28	9pm.	Nothing special to note; sick rate about the same; health of unit good. W.R.M.	REF MAP 57C. F.10 & 4.4. FRANCE 1/40,000
	29	9pm.	Visited posts and found all satisfactory. W.R.M.	
	30	9pm.	Visited CAMP MARLY D.R.S.; 44 patients still in hospital; camp clean and all patients clearing beginning of month; nothing special to note. W.R.M.	
	31	9pm.	Health of unit during the month good; the Sulpho-TURKISH bath treatment of Scabies efficacious; very few returns; suggested to A.D.M.S that blankets of BRIGADE should be disinfected whilst in reserve and so prevent re-infection. The Sulpho-Turkish bath treatment for Scabies appears to have been efficacious for cases of BOILS; very few cases of diarrhoea reported.	

W. R. Matthews
Lt-Col. R.A.M.C.T.
OC 1/3 East Lancs Fd. Amb^ce^.
42nd Div^n^.

2449 Wt. W14957/M90 750,000 1/16 J.B.C. & A. Forms/C.2118/12.

Army Form C. 2118.

WAR DIARY
or
INTELLIGENCE SUMMARY
(Erase heading not required.)

Instructions regarding War Diaries and Intelligence Summaries are contained in F. S. Regs., Part II. and the Staff Manual respectively. Title Pages will be prepared in manuscript.

Place	Date	Hour	Summary of Events and Information	Remarks and references to Appendices
~~[illegible]~~ ROYAULCOURT	31.V.17		Summary of sick & wounded passed through Field Ambulance during the month	
			Sick – 925 of these 412 were transferred to CRS & DRS & 213 to CCS.	
			Infectious diseases 2	App 12
			Venereal " " 11	
			Acc & SI wounds 18	
			Wounded 90 of these { 6 were transferred to CRS & DRS & 81 to CCS. { 3 died of wounds	
			Scabies Cases treated during month 316.	
			Cases returned for further treatment 20.	
			All cases returned were sent within a few days varying from 1–7 – sufficient time was not given to see whether cured or not. In my experience of these cases it is only after 10–14 days that one can definitely say whether cured or not.	App 13
			Procedure. The patients are first given a bath & well lathered with soap & water special attention being paid to flexures & between fingers & toes. The lather is then washed off & they are immediately introduced into the steam bath cabinet, the head protruding through a hole in the roof. Steam is now introduced & the temperature allowed to rise to 100°–106 F – this temperature is kept up for 5 minutes & the patients sweat profusely. After five minutes a burning sulphur candle is introduced	App 14

Instructions regarding War Diaries and Intelligence Summaries are contained in F. S. Regs., Part II. and the Staff Manual respectively. Title Pages will be prepared in manuscript.

WAR DIARY
or
INTELLIGENCE SUMMARY

(Erase heading not required.)

Army Form C. 2118.

Place	Date	Hour	Summary of Events and Information	Remarks and references to Appendices
			introduced through a door in the front. After 5 minutes steam is cut off. Another 20 minutes is allowed to elapse. Then the patients are removed & briskly rubbed down. They are then dressed in fresh underclothing. The uniform etc is treated [illegible] [illegible] during this period & disinfected by putting in sulphur box along with the man. After an hours rest the man is returned to his unit.	App 14
			The apparatus required is as follows:- 2 wooden cabinets each to accommodate 2 patients. Flannel [illegible] by felt each cabinet with a door at each end & 2 holes in the roof through which the patients head protrudes: & a small door in centre in front for introduction of sulphur candle - a thermometer is fixed in roof of each cabinet. Steam is furnished by means of an oil drum, steam being led into the boxes by means of 1" tubing.	
			A Callam	

2449 Wt. W14957/M90 750,000 1/16 J.B.C. & A. Forms/C.2118/12.

SECRET.

Copy No. 2

App I

ROYAL ARMY MEDICAL CORPS 42nd DIVISION ORDER No.8.

Reference Maps FRANCE 1/40,000
Sheets. 62.C. & 62.D.

5th May, 1917.

1. Headquarters Section 1/1st East Lancs Field Ambulance will move from TEMPLEUX LA FOSSE to VILLERS FAUCON on 8th inst and establish an Advanced Dressing Station at that place.

2. 1/1st East Lancs Field Ambulance will hand over to 1/2nd East Lancs Field Ambulance the dressing station at TEMPLEUX LA FOSSE.

3. 1/2nd East Lancs Field Ambulance will move one bearer subdivision to TEMPLEUX LA FOSSE from PERONNE on 8th inst and take over the dressing station from 1/1st East Lancs Field Ambulance.
They will form this into a Main Dressing and on 8th inst will move the Headquarters Tent Subdivision and two Bearer Subdivisions (less detachment at TINCOURT) to TEMPLEUX LA FOSSE.
On the 8th inst the Main Dressing Station at PERONNE will be closed and will be opened at TEMPLEUX LA FOSSE.

4. After the 8th inst no more cases will be sent to Divisional Rest Station at CAMP MARLY.

5. 1/2nd East Lancs Field Ambulance will arrange to leave one Tent Subdivision at CAMP MARLY and one Tent Subdivision at PERONNE.

6. On 8th inst the Dressing Station at PERONNE will be formed into a temporary Divisional Rest Station.

7. Completion of moves to be notified to A.D.M.S. by Motor Cyclist.

Issued at 11 a.m.
By Despatch Rider ~~D.R.L.S.~~
As follows :-
Copy No.1 to 1/1st E.L.Fld Ambce.
" " 2 " 1/2nd E.L.Fld Ambce.
" " 3 " 1/3rd E.L.Fld Ambce.
" " 4 " D.D.M.S.,IIIrd Corps.
" " 5 War Diary.
" " 6 File.

Geo Walker [signature]
Captain,
D. A. D. M. S.,42nd Division.

SECRET.

Copy No..2..........

OPERATION ORDER No. 1.

by

Major A. Callam Cmdg. 1/2nd.E.Lancs. Field Ambulance.

May 5th 1917.

Reference Map.
France 1/40,000.
Sheet 62C and 62 D.

1. "B" Section Bearer Sub-Division under the Command of Captain Gibson will move from PERONNE to TEMPLEUX LA FOSSE on 6-5-17 and take over Dressing Station there from 1/1st E.L. Field Ambce. Move to be completed by 10.a.m. They will form this into a M.D.S. to be ready for occupation by 8-5-17.

2. "A" Section under the command of Captain Purves will move complete with transport from Camp Marley on 8-5-17. Mid-day halt will be made at PERONNE. "C" Section Bearer Sub Division less detachment at TINCOURT will move with "A" Section from PERONNE to TEMPLEUX LA FOSSE. Move to be completed by 6.p.m.
3 Daimler Cars and 1 Ford will be stationed at TEMPLEUX LA FOSSE.

3. "B" Section Tent Sub-Division under command of Major Pritchard will continue to run D.R.S., Camp Marley but will not receive patients after 8-5-17. 2 Daimler Cars will be left with this party.

4. "C" Section Tent Sub-Division under command of Captain Webster will continue as M.D.S. at PERONNE until 6.p.m. 8-5-17 when it will be formed into a temporary Divisional Rest Station. 2 Daimler Cars and 1 Ford will be left with this party.

5. SCABIES. Personnel employed in this treatment will remain at PERONNE until further orders.

6. Detachment at TINCOURT will continue to evacuate to PERONNE. A Horse Ambulance wagon will be stationed at TINCOURT for this purpose. Additional transport may be obtained from PERONNE if required. Evacuations from this detachment will continue as at present up to 6.p.m. 8-5-17 after that time to M.D.S. TEMPLEUX LA FOSSE.

7. RATIONS
(a) All parties will carry 1 days rations when moving.
(b) For D.R.S. CAMP MARLEY, will be indented for sepatately.and drawn as at present.
(c) For remainder of unit will be delivered at PERONNE up to and including 8-5-17 afterwards at TEMPLEUX LA FOSSE. Rations to detachments will be distributed from these centres. "C" Section will send transport to TEMPLEUX LA FOSSE daily after 8-5-17 to draw rations for D.R.S. PERONNE to arrive 12 noon.

8. ~~Notification~~ Completion of all moves to be ~~made~~ reported at once to Field Ambulance Headquarters.

Issued at........

A Callam
Major.R.A.M.C.T.
a/O.C.1/2nd.E.Lancs. Field Ambulance.

No.1 copy File.
2 copy War Diary.
3 copy Major Pritchard.
4 copy Capt.Purves.
5 copy Capt.Gibson.
6 copy Capt.Turner.
7 copy A.D.M.S.

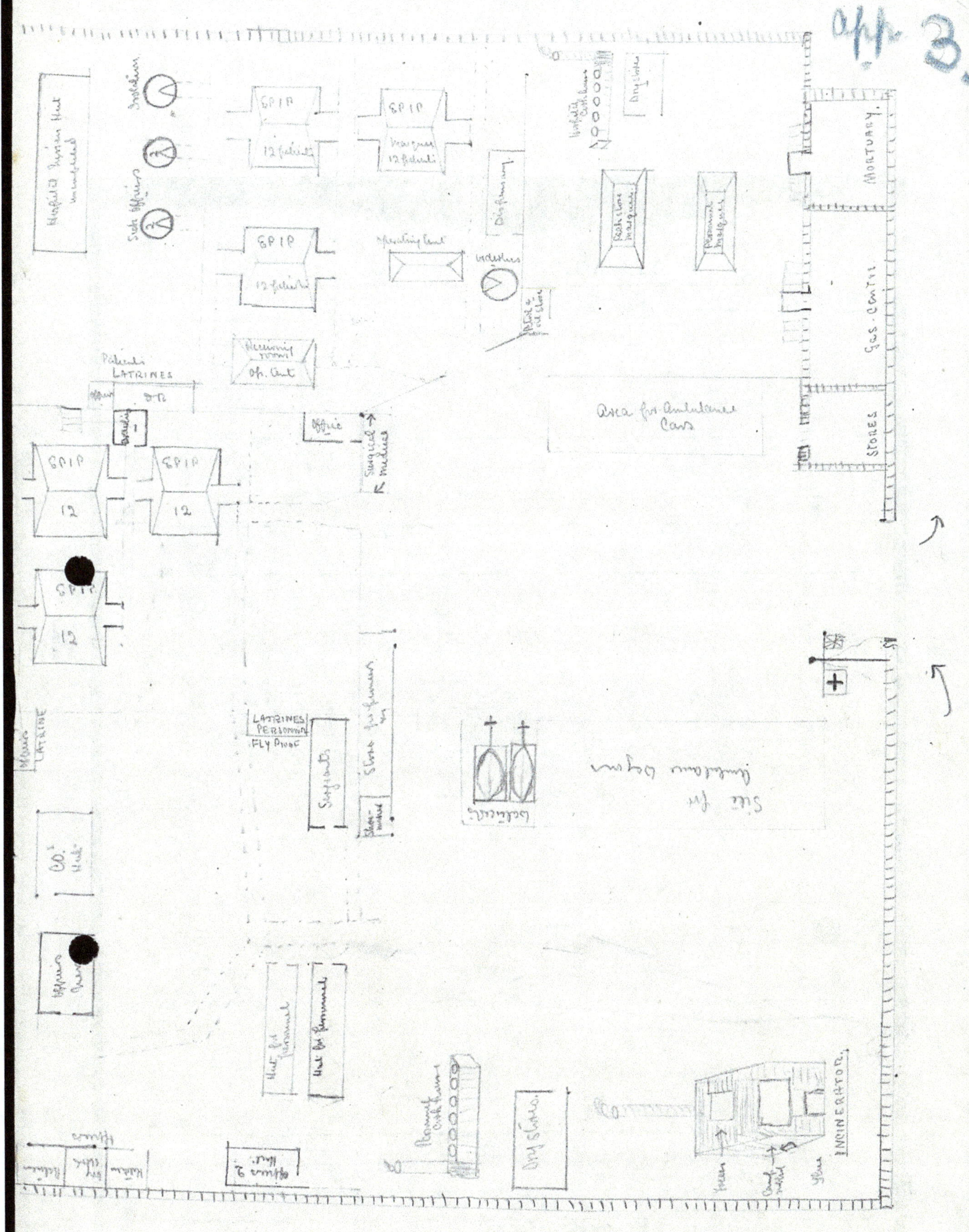

DIVISIONAL MAIN DRESSING STATION

TEMPLEUX LA FOSSE.

16·5·14

"A" Form.

Army Form C.2121 (in pads of 100).

No. of Message ....

MESSAGES AND SIGNALS.

Prefix ...... Code ...... m.	Words	Charge	This message is on a/c of:	Recd. at ......m.
Office of Origin and Service Instructions.	Sent		865/12 Service.	Date ....
	At ....m.			From ....
	To			
	By		(Signature of "Franking Officer.")	By ....

TO { O.C. 1/2nd E L Fd Amb

Sender's Number.	Day of Month.	In reply to Number.	AAA
* M421	14	✓	

Evacuate all sick from Rest Station at PERONNE to rest station at Camp MARLY to-morrow 15th inst. aaa Addressed 1/2nd Fd Amb repeated 42nd Divisional Rest station Camp MARLY

From ADMS

Place 42nd Div

Time 4 45

The above may be forwarded as now corrected.

(Z) [signature] Colonel

Censor. Signature of Addressor or person authorised to telegraph in his name.

* This line should be erased if not required.

750,000. W 2186—M509. H. W. & V., Ld. 6/16.

SECRET

Operation order No 1A Copy No 2.

Major Cullam Comdg. 1/2nd E. Yd. Amb.

5

Ref 62C. 1/40000. 14. 5. 17

Moves. – The following move will take place tomorrow 15. 5. 17

DRS. PERONNE will be evacuated & personnel–less those employed in Scabies treatment will move to TEMPLEUX LA FOSSE. D28 d

Instructions (1) Evacuation of Patients

(a) Patients not likely to be fit within 7 days will be sent to CCS.

(b) Patients likely to be fit within 7 days will be sent to DRS. Camp MARLY.

(c) Scabies cases will continue to be treated at PERONNE until further orders

(d) Any cases of Venereal or S I W. detained pending investigation will be sent to MDS.

(2) Records & ~~A & D books~~

These will be sent to Camp MARLY immediately cases have been evacuated.

A clerk will be detailed from PERONNE for temporary assistance at Camp MARLY.

All returns &c will be sent direct to ADMS from Camp MARLY through his office by 2 PM daily

Secret. Operation Order No 3 Copy No 2

by

Major Callam Comdg 1/7th [illegible]

Billeting party – Capt. Selon + 1 NCO

will report to [illegible] 30th Divn

at P 26 b 5.0 (Map 57C 1–40000)

[illegible] 12 noon

Rations. The unexpended portion of days rations + rations for the following day will be carried

Blankets will be carried

Issued at 12.45 pm

A Callam Major
Cmdg 1/7th [illegible]

No 1 Copy Filed

2 . Bde [illegible]

3 Capt Selon[illegible]

Sheet 2.

(3) Evacuation from DRS Camp MARLY

(a) ~~there~~ will take place as previously laid down.

(b) As far as possible no further cases will be sent to Camp MARLY.

(c) No vacancies will be allotted for CRS CERISY, except there are insufficient cases at MDS to fill vacancies

(4) Rations - OC DRS PERONNE will arrange to send 2 days rations with patients to Camp MARLY.

(5) MOVE to TEMPLEUX LA FOSSE will be completed by 10 am 16.5.17.

For transport of extra blankets stretchers etc a GS wagon will be sent from MDS.

(6) Reports of completion of evacuation of patients will be forwarded at once to MDS.

(7) MARKING of SITE at PERONNE. OC DRS PERONNE will notify Town Major before moving out & will put up notice boards indicating that the Camp is "reserved as FD Amb site".

Issued at 10-15 Pm 14.5.17.

No 1 Copy file
2 War Diary
3 OC DRS Camp MARLY
4 OC DRS PERONNE

[illegible] Major

Secret  Copy No. 2

ADDENDUM
TO
ROYAL ARMY MEDICAL CORPS 42nd DIVISION ORDER No.9.

Reference Maps FRANCE 1/40,000
Sheets 57.c.and 62.c.

19th May, 1917.

Second half of paragraph 5 is cancelled. On 20th inst. Headquarters Section and one tent sub-division will proceed by route march to BUS (57.c.O.24) route Mt St QUENTIN - HAUT ALLAINES - MOISLAINS - MANANCOURT ETRICOURT - LECHELLE and take over site from 61st Field Ambulance and prepare to receive sick.

One bearer sub-division will proceed by march route via NURLU and FINS to DESSART area and join the 125th Brigade group under orders of 125th Brigade group.

[signature]
Colonel,
A.D.M.S.,42nd Division.

Distribution as for Order No.9.

SECRET. Copy No. 2

ROYAL ARMY MEDICAL CORPS 42nd DIVISION ORDER No.9

Reference Maps FRANCE, 1/40,000
Sheets 62.c.,62.d.,57.c.

15th May, 1917.

1. The 2nd Cavalry Division (less artillery relieves the 42nd Division (less artillery) on the nights May 16th/17th to 18th/19th both inclusive.
Each Brigade on relief will concentrate in the Reserve Brigade area and march to XVth Corps area from there.

2. The Reserve Brigade area comprises LONGAVESNES,VILLERS FAUCON,SAULCOURT, and Camp K.11 central.
YTRES area comprises NEUVILLE-BOURJONVAL, RUYAULCOURT, BERTINCOURT and YTRES.
DESSART area comprises EQUANCOURT, FINS, DESSART WOOD and camps in the vicinity.

3. The 1/2nd East Lancs Field Ambulance (less detachments at PERONNE and CAMP MARLY) will be relieved by a Field Ambulance of 2nd Cavalry Division on 16th inst and on relief will remain at TEMPLEUX LA FOSSE.
The detachment of 1/2nd East Lancs Field Ambulance at PERONNE will join the 1/2nd East Lancs Field Ambulance at TEMPLEUX LA FOSSE on 16th inst.
The detachment of 1/2nd East Lancs Field Ambulance forming the Divisional Rest Station at CAMP MARLY will remain where it is until further orders.
On 17th inst 1/2nd East Lancs Field Ambulance less One detachment will move with 127th Brigade group under orders of 127th Brigade group to YTRES area, joining the Brigade group at LIERAMONT from TEMPLEUX LA FOSSE at an hour to be notified by G.O.C., 127th Brigade. Route :- LIERAMONT-NURLU-ETRICOURT.

4. The 1/1st East Lancs Field Ambulance will be relieved by Field Ambulances of 2nd Cavalry Division on the night 17th/18th inst and will remain in the Reserve Brigade area.
On 19th inst it will march with 126th Brigade group under orders of 126th Brigade group to DESSART area clearing the Reserve Brigade area by 6 a.m.. Route :- LIERAMONT-NURLU-FINS.
On 20th inst it will move with the Brigade group from DESSART area to YTRES area under orders of 126th Brigade group

ammendments added

5. 1/3rd East Lancs Field Ambulance (less one section at CERISY) after relief by a Field Ambulance of 59th Division will remain at DOINGT until 20th inst.

~~On 20th inst it will proceed by march route via NURLU and FINS to DESSART area and join the 125th Brigade group under orders of 125th Brigade group.~~ Cancelled

6. When on the march distances of 400 yards will be kept between Batteries Battalions etc.

All motor transport will move via ST DENIS-HAUT ALLAINES-MANANCOURT-ROCQUIGNY YTRES.

7. On arrival in the XVth Corps area the 42nd Division will be required to relieve the 20th Division on a three Brigade front starting probably on the night 19th/20th May.

Separate orders will be issued for this relief.

8. Evacuation of sick will be as under:-

While in 111rd Corps area to Main dressing Station 2nd Cavalry Division TEMPLEUX LA FOSSE.

When in XVth Corps area to Corps Main dressing station FINS.

9. A.D.M.S. Office will close at K.11.a.7.0. at 9 a.m. on 19th inst and open at the same hour at FLAMICOURT (Peronne).

Issued at 3.30 p.m.
By Despatch Rider D.R.L.S.
As follows :-

Copy No.1 1/1st E.L.Fld Ambce.
" " 2 1/2nd E.L.Fld Ambce.
" " 3 1/3rd E.L.Fld Ambce.
" " 4 D.D.M.S.,111rd Corps.
" " 5 D.D.M.S.,XVth Corps.
" " 6 A.D.M.S.,2nd Cavalry Divn.
" " 7 File.
" " 8 War Diary.

Geo Dalziel.
Captain,
D. A. D. M. S.,42nd Division.

OC 1/2nd E.L. Fld. Ambce.

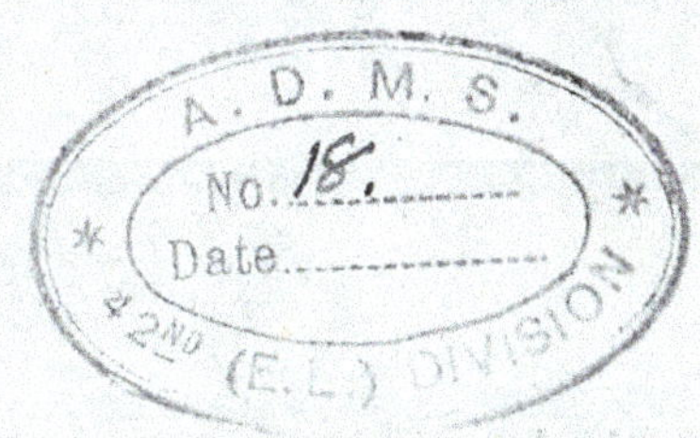

=====================

Reference R.A.M.C.,42nd Division Order No.9 of 15th inst.

A.D.M.S. Office will open on 19th inst at BRUSLE J.34.b. and not at FLAMICOURT.

18/5/17.

Captain,
D.A.D.M.S., 42nd Division.

Distribution :- as for Order No.9.

SECRET & URGENT.

To/

O.C., 1/2nd Fld Ambulance

You will be attached to this Brigade for a move into a new area, and will be required to move very early on morning of 17th May.

Orders will follow.

Captain,
Brigade Major,
127th Infy.Brigade.

SECRET & URGENT

HEADQUARTERS,
127TH
INFANTRY BRIGADE.
No. BMR/484
Date 15/5/17

To/
O.C., 1/2nd East Lancs Fld Ambce

Billetting parties as under will report to the D.A.A.&Q.M.G., 20th Division, at 20th Division Hd. Qrs. at P.26,b.50 (Map 57c 1:40,000) at 12 noon to-morrow.

They should take rations for the 17th and a Blanket with them and be mounted on bycicles or horses.

		Off.	N.C.Os.
Battalion.	(1 Officer per Battalion)	4	
Company.	(1 N.C.O. per Coy)		16
127th M.G.COy.		1	1
127th T.M.B.		1	1
427th Fld Coy R.E.		1	1
1/2nd East Lancs Fld Ambce.		1+	1 +
Bde Sig: Section.			1
451st Divnl.Train.		1	1
		9	22

Orders for move follow.

[signature]

Captain,
Brigade Major,
127th Infy.Brigade.

SECRET.

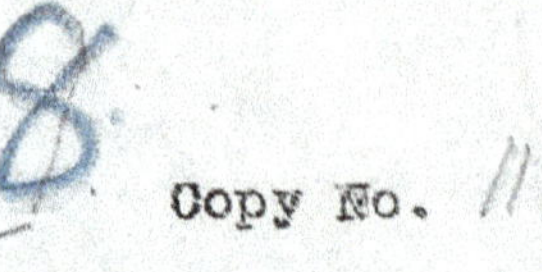

Copy No. 11

127TH INFANTRY BRIGADE ORDER NO.15.

REF: Maps 1:40,000 62c and 57c. 16/5/17.

1. The Brigade and attached troops will move in accordance with attached march table from this area to the area YTRES, NEUVILLE BOURGONVILLE, ROYAULCOURT, BERTINCOURT on the 17th inst, preparatory to taking over a Brigade front EAST of that area on the 19th inst.

2. The following are attached to the Brigade for the move :-

   1/2nd East Lancs Field Ambulance.
   427th Fld Coy. R.E.
   431st Coy. Divnl. Train.

3. The orders re intervals of a 100 yards between platoons will not hold good for this march.
   The following intervals will be kept on the march:-

   10 yards between Companies.
   400 " " Battalions.
   400 " " M.G. Coy and other Units.
   400 " " Field Coy R.E. and other Units.
   100 " " each Units Transport.

   The M.G.Coy and T.M.Battery will march as one Unit.

4. TRANSPORT Lewis Gun Limbers and cookers will march in rear of their Companies.
   The 12 Machine Gun G.S. Limbers will march with the M.G. Coy.
   Field Coy.R.E. and Field Ambulance Transport will march with their Units.
   The remaining Transport of the Brigade will rendezvous in order of march, in Units on the LIERAMONT - VILLERS FAUCON Road. Head of Column will pass cross roads E.14.b.9.2. at 5-40a.m.

5. Halts will be made at the clock hours for 10 minutes. Packs will be removed; mounted men will dismount, and men will fall out on the right hand side and clear of the road during halts.
   There will be a halt of one hour and 10 minutes from 8 a.m. to 9.10 a.m.

6. O.C. 1/7th Bn.Manchester Regt will detail One Platoon under an Officer to march in rear of the Transport to collect stragglers, and to take the names of any men who have fallen out without written permission from their Unit.
   The 2nd East Lancs Field Ambulance will detail a Medical Officer to accompany this party. He will decide if men who have fallen out are fit to march or whether they should be carried in the Ambulance wagons.

7. Rations for the 18th inst will be taken to Units billeting areas after arrival, under supply arrangements.

/ continued.

/continued.

8. Steel helmets will be worn by all ranks in possession.

9. Marching out states will reach Brigade H.Q. by 8 p.m. to-day.

10. Move complete reports will be furnished to Brigade Hd.Qrs. YTRES as soon as possible after arrival.

11. Reports to Head of Main Body.

Captain,
Brigade Major,
127th Infy Brigade.

Issued at 8.30 a.m.
By. Orderly
~~DRLS~~

Copy No.1 - 1/5th Manchesters.
" " 2 - 1/6th "
" " 3 - 1/7th "
" " 4 - 1/8th "
" " 5 - 127th M.G.Coy.
" " 6 - 127th T.M.B.
" " 7 - 42nd Division.
" " 8 - 20th Division.
" " 9 - C.R.E., 42nd Div.
" "10 - 427th Fld Coy.R.E.
" "11 - 1/2nd East Lancs Fld Ambce.
" "12 - 431st Coy. Divnl.Train.
" "13 - Staff Captain.
" "14 - Bde Transport Officer.
" "15 - " Signalling "
" "16 - " Supply "
" "17)
" "18) - War Diary.
" "19 - File.

MARCH TABLE.

to accompany 127th Infantry Brigade Order No.15. 16/5/17.

Units in order of march.	Time to pass starting point.	Starting Point.	Destination (Sheet 57c)	Route.	Remarks.
127th Bde H.Q. & Sig. Section.	5.5. a.m.	Junction of roads West of LIERAMONT at D. 12. c. 7. 2. (Sheet 62c).	YTRES (P.20)	LIERAMONT - NURLU - MANANCOURT ETRICOURT - P.32. - YTRES. from whence Units will march independently to their respective Billeting areas.	Units will not pass cross roads E.14. b. prior to the Unit preceding them in order of march.
8th Manchesters. (Eighth)	5.10.a.m.		RUYAULCOURT (P.10.)		
6th Manchesters.	5.20a.m.		NEUVILLE BOURJONVAL (P.22)		
5th Manchesters.	5.30.a.m.		BERTINCOURT (P.7.)		
7th Manchesters.	5.40.a.m.		YTRES (P.20)		
127th T.M.B.) 127th M.G.Coy.)	5.50.a.m.		NEUVILLE BOURJONVAL (P.22.) YTRES (P.20).		
427th Fld. Coy R.E.	6.10.a.m.		Billeting area not yet known, will be met by guides.		
Brigade Transport.	6.20.a.m.		Units areas.		
Field Ambce.	7.10.a.m.		Probably RUYAULCOURT but guides will meet them.		
431st Coy.Divnl Train.	-		Not yet known, will be met by guides.		Will march under the orders of O.C. Company.

To 1/2nd E.L. Fld Ambce

SECRET

AMMENDMENT TO 127th INFANTRY BRIGADE ORDER No. 18

Billeting Areas will be as under :-

Bde. H.Q. - ~~XXXXX~~ YTRES

5th Manchesters - BERTINCOURT

6th Manchesters - YTRES

7th MANCHESTERS - VALLULART WOOD

8th Manchesters - ROYAULCOURT

127th M.G. Coy. - Neuville

127th T.M.B. - NEUVILLE

427th Field Coy. R.E. - NEUVILLE

2nd Field Amb. -BERTINCOURT

431st Coy. A.S.C.- YTRES.

On arrival the following can send to Bde . H.Q. for extra tentage :-

7th Manchesters

8th Manchesters

6th Manchesters (if unable to find sufficient accommodation)

W.T. Woods Captain,
Staff Captain,
127th Infantry Brigade.

16/5/17

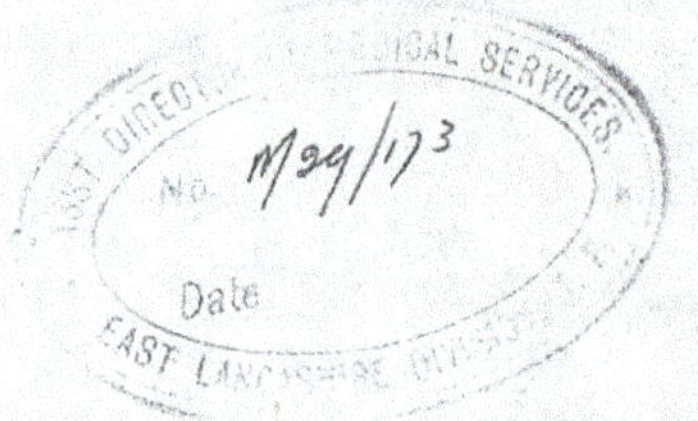

O.C.,
1/2nd E.L.Field Ambulance.

The following extracts from 42nd Division Administrative Instructions No.2 are forwarded for your information and necessary action :-

4. A dump for the Division will be formed in an Adrian Hut at VILLERS FAUCON. All stores etc., surplus to what can be carried on baggage wagons, and for which additional transport cannot be immediately obtained, will be stored there.

A guard will be provided on the following scale :-

1 Officer from each Infantry Brigade.
1 Officer from R.A.
1 storeman from each unit.
All ranks of this party will be provided with 7 days rations.

8. Area Commandants will be relieved at a date to be notified later, by Officers of the Cavalry Corps, and will proceed on relief to take over areas from 20th Division as follows :-

Commandant.	From.	To.	Relieving.
2/Lt.WALTON, 6th Manchesters.	No.1 Area	Bertincourt-Royaulcourt area	Captain J.LATHAM, 6th K.S.L.I.
2/Lt.L.S.BERGL 5th Lan.Fus.	No.2 "	Neuville area	2/Lt.F.C.KIRBY, 11th R.B.
2/Lt.C.SCHULTZ, 5th Lan.Fus.	No.3 "	Ytres area	Lt.C.B.WEBSTER. 11th K.R.R.C.
2/Lt.H.B.SILVERWOOD 6th Lan.Fus.	4 "	Bus-Lechelle area	Lt.A.B.STEVENSON 12th Kings.
2/Lt.J.C.MORTON 7th Manchesters	No.5 "	Rocquigny & Les Mesnil.	2/Lt.F.E.WILLCOCK, 7th ~~Somerset~~ D.C. L.I.
2/Lt.H.H.NIGHT 9th Manchesters		Barastre- Le Transloy.	2/Lt.J.H.GOODE, 7th Somerset L.I.
Lt.M.STEAD 5th E.Lancs.		Metz-En Coutre.	Lt.Brandon-Powell, 12th K.R.R.C.

Area Commandants will take their clerks and Batmen with them.

126th Infantry Brigade will detail one clerk for each New Area Commandant to be founs by them.

16/5/17.

[signature]
Captain,
D. A. D. M. S.,42nd Division.

SECRET.   A.I.3.

MOVE of 42ND DIVISION.

CONTINUATION OF ADMINISTRATIVE INSTRUCTIONS.

1. TRANSPORT. The following wagons will be placed at the disposal of the undermentioned Units at 5 p.m. on the 16th inst., at VILLERS FAUCON Church and will be met there by guides of Units concerned.

127th Brigade	- 6 wagons from D.A.C.
427th Field Coy.R.E.	- 2 wagons from 42nd Div.Train.
2nd Field Ambulance	- 1 G.S.wagon from 42nd Div.Train.
127th Brigade	- 4 motor lorries from 42nd D.S.C.

All the above wagons will proceed to YTRES on the 17th inst. and will return to the D.A.C. and Train on the 18th inst. They will take rations for 17th and 18th.
The motor lorries will return to PERONNE on the night of the 17th.
The baggage wagons of the 127th Brigad e and the 427th Field Coy. R.E. will be placed at their disposal by noon on the 16th.

The Brigade will make its own arrangements for transport for move from YTRES to forward area on 18th inst.

2. RATIONS. The Brigade will move with rations for 17th on man and for 18th on Supply wagons.
6 motor lorries will be at the disposal of S.S.O. on 17th inst. and will take rations for 19th from ROISEL to YTRES.
Brigade will make its own arrangements for refilling at YTRES. Motor lorries to rejoin the Supply Column, PERONNE on night 17th inst.
YTRES will remain the Refilling Point for 127th Brigade.

3. GARFORD LORRIES. Para.7. of Administrative Instructions A.I.2. of 15th inst. is cancelled.

4. PACK SADDLERY. Surplus to Moblization Equipment will be handed in to 111 Corps Ordnance, PERONNE.

5. AMMUNITION. The Trench Mortar Battery will take 110 rounds with it. Any other Trench Mortar Ammunition will be returned to the A.R.P.

A statement showing amount and description of all ammunition taken to be rendered to D.H.Q. by the 19th inst.

[signature]

16/5/17.

Captain,
for Lt.Colonel,
A.A.& Q.M.G.
42nd Division

C.R.A.
C.R.E.
127th Bde.
42nd Div.Train.
42nd Supply Col.
A.D.M.S.
D.A.D.O.S.
20th Division.
G.

O.C. 1/2nd E.L. Fd Amb.

For information & necessary action

16/5/17

Geo Dalziel
Col/Lt
DADMS
[illegible]

To:O.C. 1/2nd Field Amb.

On arrival at their new billets units will arrange to meet their baggage wagons at the cross roads at P. 20.b.70., map 57c. Guides for Supply Wagons must be sent toBrigade Headquarters near the cemetery at YTRES.

All wagons should be returned to 451st Coy. A.S.C. as early as possible. at Ytres.

W. D. Woods Captain,
Staff Captain,
127th Infy. Brigade.

16/5/17

9 10

SECRET.

Copy No. 2

ROYAL ARMY MEDICAL CORPS 42nd DIVISION ORDER No.10.

Reference Maps FRANCE, 1/40,000
Sheet 57.c.

16th May, 1917.

1. The 42nd Division relieves the 20th Division now holding the front HAVRINCOURT WOOD - VILLERS PLUICH starting on the night 19th/20th and completing on the night 24th/25th.

The 20th Division front is held by three Brigades in the line each Brigade with three Battalions in the line.

2. Infantry Brigades will relieve as follows :-

42nd Div.		20th Div.		Date.	Trench Sector.
Bdes. relieving.	Field Coy.	Bde relieving	Field Coy.	May.	
127th	427th	61st	84th	19/20	Left.
126th	428th	59th	96th	21/22	Centre.
125th	429th	60th	83rd	22/23	Right.

3. Field Ambulances will relieve as follows :-

42nd Div. Fld Ambs.	20th Div. Fld.Ambs.	Date. May	Place.
1/2nd E.Lan.	61st	19th	Adv.Dr.Stn.at RUYAULCOURT.
1/1st E.Lan.	H.Q.& part 62nd	21st.	Adv.Dr.Stn.at NEUVILLE.
1/3rd E.Lan.	Part 62nd	22nd	Adv.Dr.Stn.at METZ (Q.20.d.2.2)

Reliefs to be completed by 6 p.m. on the dates given.

4. 1/2nd E.Lancs Field Ambulance will evacuate sick and wounded from the left trench sector occupied by 127th Brigade.

1/1st E.Lancs Field Ambulance will evacuate sick and wounded from the centre trench sector occupied by 126th Brigade.

1/3rd E.Lancs Field Ambulance will evacuate sick and wounded from the right trench sector occupied by 125th Brigade.

Reliefs to be arranged between O's C. Field Ambulances.

5. Lines of evacuation will be the same as carrie out by 20th Division.

6. A.D.M.S. Office will close at FLAMICOURT (PERONNE) and open at LITTLE WOOD south of YTRES (P.28.b.5.9) at 10 a.m. on May 23rd.

Issued at 9 p.m.
By Despatch Rider ~~D.R.L.S.~~
As follows :-

Copy No. 1 1/1st E.L.Fld Ambce.
" " 2 1/2nd E.L.Fld Ambce.
" " 3 1/3rd E.Lan.Fld Ambce.
" " 4 D.D.M.S.,111rd Corps.
" " 5 D.D.M.S.,XVth Corps.
" " 6 A.D.M.S.,20th Div.
" " 7 War Diary.
" " 8 File.

G Dalziel
Captain,
D. A. D. M. S.,42nd Division

app 10.

SECRET.

Copy No..5.....

Field Ambulance Operation Orders No.2.
By Major. A. Callam R.A.M.C.T.
A/O.C. 1/2nd. East Lancashire Field Ambulance.

Ref. Sheet 57c 1/20,000

This Field Ambulance will relieve the 61st. Field Ambulance A.D.S. at RUYAULCOURT Map Ref. P10.c.85 and evacuate the Left Brigade Sector and Left Half of Central Brigade Sector (HAVRINCOURT WOOD) move to be completed by 6 p.m. on the 19th inst.

Details.1

1 N.C.O. and 16 other Ranks from B & C Bearer sub Divisions will be at RUYALCOURT by 12.30 noon to-day and will relieve the corrssponding number of Men of 61st Field Amb. in the line-relief to be arranged by the C.O. A.D.S. RUYAULCOURT

2.

Capt. C.A. Webster and Capt. W.Turner along with "C" Section Tent Sub Division will form a Dressing Station at RUYAULCOURT, will take over the working of that post by 3.p.m.

3.

Capt. W.Turner will take over the A.D.S. Equipment and Stores by time arranged.

4.

Capt. Purves will arrange the Bearer Posts and Evacuations from the Line.

5.

The Transport of "C" Section will move with Tent Sub Div. Cooks Waggon and necessary utensils will move with this party.

6.

WORKING PARTIES

1 N.C.O. and 20 Men for erecting accomadation for personnel to be drawn from "A" Section will move ~~fm~~ with "C" Section. 8 Bell Tents and 2 Tarpaulins will be at the disposal of this party .

7.

Sergt. Duckworth 8 Men from "B" Section and 24 Men from "C" Section will march off at 11 a.m. on 19-5-17 to take over Bearer Posts Duties. Two Wheeled Stretchers will be taken by this party.

8.

Two Ford Card Will be at RUYAULCOURT at 12 noon,each Car will carry Four Petrol Tins full of Water and one Tank from each Ambulance Waggon (B & C Section)

9.

Remainder of Unit will be at RUYAULCOURT at 6.p.m.

10.

RATIONS.

All parties will move with the unexpended portion of days rations on Man.

Issued at 9.a.m.
18-5-17

A Callam
Major. R.A.M.C.T.
A/O.C. 1/2nd. E.Lancs. Field Amb

No 1 Copy A.D.M.S.
2 " Capt. Purves.
3 " " Webster.
4 " " Turner.
5 " War Diary
6 2 File.

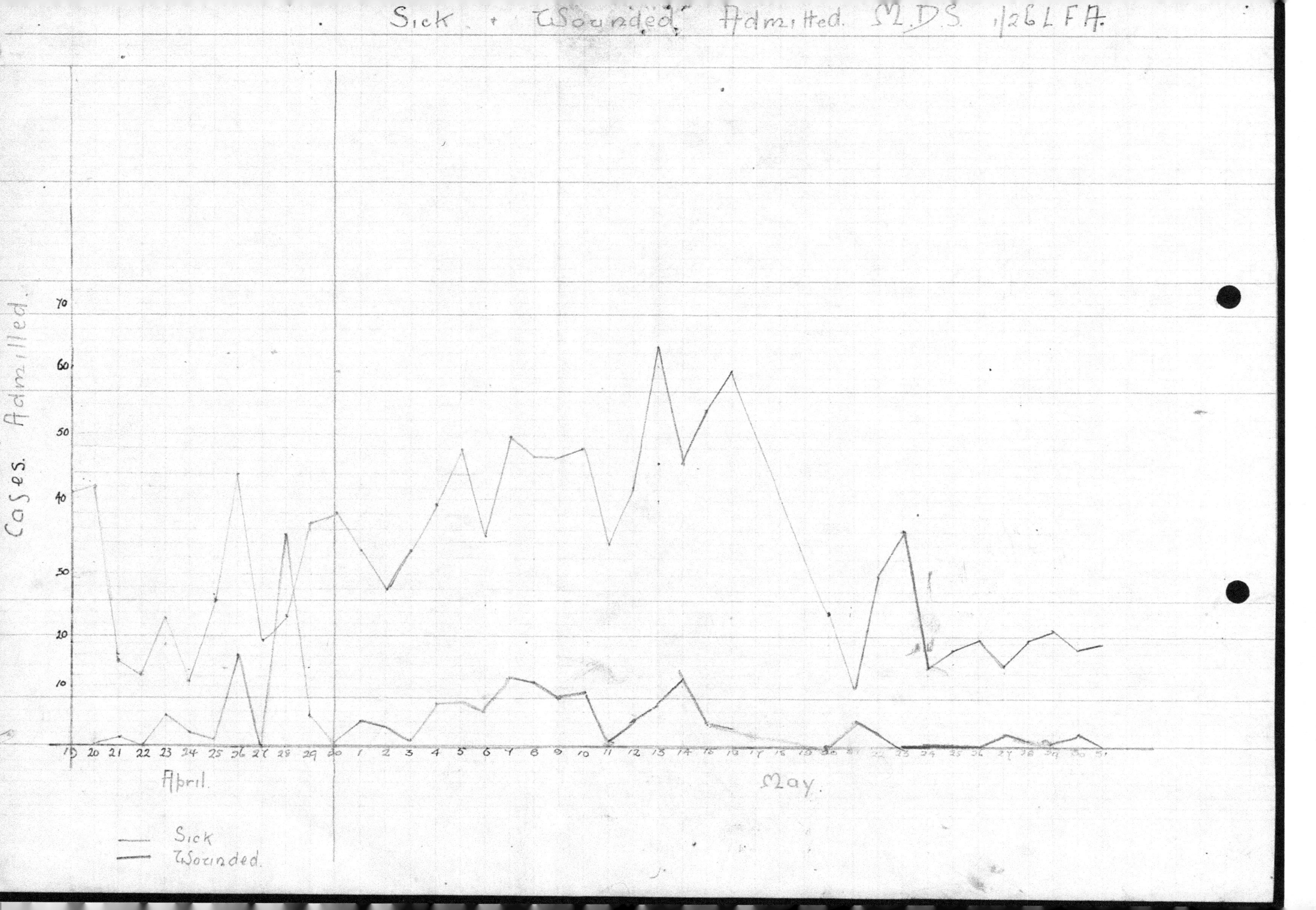
Sick + Wounded Admitted. M.D.S. 1/2 L F A.
Cases. Admitted.
70
60
50
40
30
20
10
19 20 21 22 23 24 25 26 27 28 29 30 1 2 3 4 5 6 7 8 9 10 11 12 13 14 15 16 17 18 19 20 21 22 23 24 25 26 27 28 29 30 31
April.
May.
Sick
Wounded.

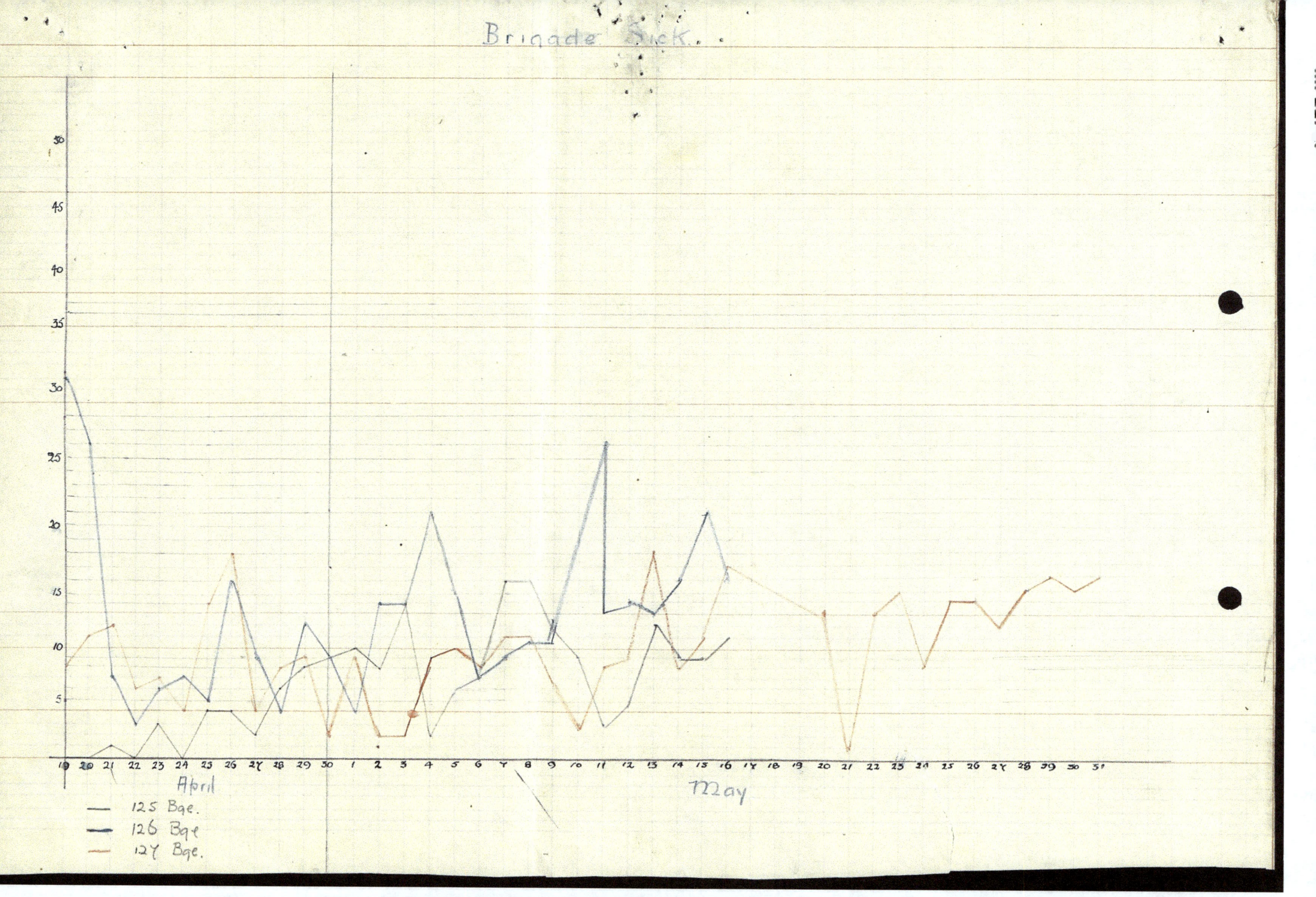
Brigade Sick.
50
45
40
35
30
25
20
15
10
5
19 20 21 22 23 24 25 26 27 28 29 30 1 2 3 4 5 6 7 8 9 10 11 12 13 14 15 16 17 18 19 20 21 22 23 24 25 26 27 28 29 30 31
April
May
125 Bge.
126 Bge
127 Bge.

Apl 12. Chart of Brigade's Sick & wounded

Scabies Cases treated at M.D.S. 1/2 E.L. F. Amb.

Cases

45 40 35 30 25 20 19 18 17 16 15 14 13 12 11 10 9 8 7 6 5 4 3 2 1

25 26 27 28 29 30 1 2 3 4 5 6 7 8 9 10 11 12 13 14 15 16 17 18 19 20 21 22 23 24 25 26 27 28 29 30 31.

April

May

Moving

App 13

Chart of Scabies Cases

CONFIDENTIAL.

WAR DIARY

OF

1/2 EAST LANC. FIELD AMBCE.

42ND DIVISION.

VOL. VI. 1 – 30 JUNE 1917.

Instructions regarding War Diaries and Intelligence Summaries are contained in F. S. Regs., Part II. and the Staff Manual respectively. Title Pages will be prepared in manuscript.

WAR DIARY

or

~~INTELLIGENCE SUMMARY~~

(Erase heading not required.)

Army Form C. 2118

Place	Date 1917 June	Hour	Summary of Events and Information	Remarks and references to Appendices
RUYAULCOURT.	1.	9pm.	Nothing special to note: visited bearer posts: found satisfactory: admissions during the last 24 hours are sick 11 wounded 22: number of sick at Marly Camp now 30. A.D.M.S. suggests moving personnel from Camp Marly on 8th inst by which time the D.R.S. will be empty. Posts manned and worked by personnel see map App. 1. W.R.M.	REF MAP 57C P.10 C 4.4 FRANCE 1/40,000.
	2.	9pm.	During the last 24 hours 29 sick and 17 wounded admitted & passed through the A.D.S.: posts visited by officers and M.O. of battalions seen. Nothing else special to note. Soup kitchens started & working well. W.R.M.	REF MAP 57C N.E 57C S.E FRANCE 1/40000
	3	9pm.	Posts visited today and things satisfactory at the several R.L.P. B.P. and L.P. The three soup kitchens are working satisfactorily and the cocoa appreciated by the men. It is essential to have it sweetened as it is more palatable but especially as the sugar is so easily assimilated & counteracts exhaustion with the men. Nothing else to note. 27 sick 21 wounded. W.R.M.	App. 1.
	4	9pm.	Nothing special to note. Issued orders for details to leave Camp Marly on the 8th by route march see App. 2. 42 sick passed through and 23 wounded during the 24 hours. W.R.M.	App. 2.
	5	9pm.	Visited posts and found everything satisfactorily: the work being carried out at R.L.P. progressing: certain improvements suggested. New hospital ward nearing completion. 33 sick admitted and 2 wounded passed through. W.R.M.	

Instructions regarding War Diaries and Intelligence Summaries are contained in F. S. Regs., Part II. and the Staff Manual respectively. Title Pages will be prepared in manuscript.

WAR DIARY

or

~~INTELLIGENCE SUMMARY~~

(Erase heading not required.)

Army Form C. 2118

Place	Date 1917 June	Hour	Summary of Events and Information	Remarks and references to Appendices
RUYAULCOURT.	6.	9pm.	Nothing special to note. Lt+Qr. M. I. M. LOWE evacuated sick to L of C suffering from acute appendicitis. 23 sick admitted and 2 wounded passed through during the last 24 hours. W.R.M.	
	7.	9pm.	Post visited today by officers and everything all right; building operations are progressing satisfactorily. Operation on Lt. Qr. LOWE today: appendix found to be gangrenous; some fluid in abdomen. It is interesting to note that the symptoms were very slight + unsuspecting at [illegible] in the night, yet the condition was so serious and operation in the nick of time. 32 patients admitted today + 7 wounded passed through the A.D.S. Captain PURVES on leave. W.R.M.	
	8.	9pm.	Post visited. work going on satisfactorily: advance party from Camp MARLY arrived by Motor Ambulance. 51 patients admitted sick and 4 passed through wounded during last 24 hours. W.R.M.	
	9	9pm.	Nothing special to note. 45 patients admitted sick and 4 passed through wounded. W.R.M.	
	10	9pm.	Nothing special. Post visited and all satisfactory. 28 patients admitted sick and 15 passed through wounded. The greatest percentage of sick is due to N.Y.D FEVER. It is suggested that this condition is due to lice infection. It seems only to affect those in the line and those associated with them coming into contact with them + so get infected. All the cases occurring in this unit have been in those posts behind the line. Details reported from CAMP MARLY. W.R.M.	

1875 Wt. W593/826 1,000,000 4/15 J.B.C. & A. A.D.S.S./Forms/C. 2118.

Instructions regarding War Diaries and Intelligence Summaries are contained in F. S. Regs., Part II. and the Staff Manual respectively. Title Pages will be prepared in manuscript.

WAR DIARY

~~or~~

~~INTELLIGENCE SUMMARY~~

(Erase heading not required.)

Army Form C. 2118

Place	Date 1919 June	Hour	Summary of Events and Information	Remarks and references to Appendices
RUYAULCOURT	11	9pm.	Nothing special to note. Work at the posts satisfactory. The making of dugouts & shell proof shelters proceeding. Hospital ward practically ready. 21 patients admitted sick during last 24 hours and 13 wounded passed through. W.R.M.	
	12	9pm.	Nothing special to note. 13 patients admitted sick and 2 wounded during the past 24 hours. Visited posts with ADMS today and RE officer with a view to forming an dugout A.D.S. Suggested site selected. W.R.M.	
	13	9pm.	Had the first case of Phosgene Gas poisoning today at 4 p.m. On arrival the patient was found in great distress from difficulty of breathing and pulse quick & irregular. Patient cyanosed, right side of heart enlarged and his lungs full of adventitious sounds but not much cough or expectoration. Injection of morphine was given and then venesection performed and 12 oz of blood removed. The blood was dark tarry looking & flowed with difficulty from the vein. After venesection his condition improved and though restless he seemed better. Ammonia ampoules were also given for inhalation. Oxygen inhalation also given. W.R.M. MAJOR CA[illegible] RAMC left the unit to command 1/1st East Lancs Fd. Amb. 13 sick and 3 wounded passed through during past 24 hours.	
	14	9pm.	Two other cases of Phosgene Gas poisoning during the past 24 hours. The same treatment adopted & venesection performed and all with good results. All the patients doing well and in all probability will recover. In my opinion venesection should be done early in every case as being the best treatment for the patient. W.R.M.	

1875 Wt. W593/826 1,000,000 4/15 J.B.C. & A. A.D.S.S./Forms/C. 2118.

Army Form C. 2118

Instructions regarding War Diaries and Intelligence Summaries are contained in F. S. Regs., Part II. and the Staff Manual respectively. Title Pages will be prepared in manuscript.

WAR DIARY
or
INTELLIGENCE SUMMARY
(Erase heading not required.)

Place	Date 1917 June	Hour	Summary of Events and Information	Remarks and references to Appendices
RUYAULCOURT.	15.	9pm.	All the patients suffering from gas poisoning done well and transferred to C.M.D.S. Venesection was performed in all these cases and is the treatment for the condition until some antidote is found. 19 sick admitted and 8 passed through the A.D.S. during past 24 hours. W.R.M.	
	16.	9pm.	Visit from D.D.M.S. III Corps today along with A.D.M.S. 42nd Div. informed he was satisfied. Posts visited & all satisfactory. 24 sick admitted and 9 wounded passed through the A.D.S. during the past 24 hours. W.R.M	
	17	9pm	Nothing special to note. 25 patients admitted sick and 8 wounded passed through the A.D.S. during past 24 hours. W.R.M.	
	18	9pm.	Nothing special to note. 27 patients sick admitted and 3 wounded passed through A.D.S. during the past 24 hours. Posts visited. W.R.M.	
	19	9pm.	Nothing special to note. Captain PURVES returned from leave. 36 sick patients admitted to Hospital + 5 passed through A.D.S. wounded. W.R.M.	
	20	9pm.	Nothing special to note. Captain Steward S.R. reported for duty with the unit. Posts visited + all satisfactory. 23 sick admitted to Hospital and 2 wounded passed through A.D.S. during last 24 hours. W.R.M.	
	21	9pm	Nothing special to note. All satisfactory. Evacuations working smoothly and the men working well. 27 sick admitted into Hospital + 7 wounded passed through. W.R.M.	

1875 Wt. W593/826 1,000,000 4/15 J.B.C. & A. A.D.S.S./Forms/C. 2118.

Army Form C. 2118

Instructions regarding War Diaries and Intelligence Summaries are contained in F. S. Regs., Part II. and the Staff Manual respectively. Title Pages will be prepared in manuscript.

WAR DIARY
~~or INTELLIGENCE SUMMARY~~
(Erase heading not required.)

Place	Date 1917 June	Hour	Summary of Events and Information	Remarks and references to Appendices
RUYAULCOURT	22	9pm	Visited posts and found all satisfactory: evacuations working smoothly. Soup Kitchens working well and appreciated by the men whom they are intended for. CAPTAIN G.B. JAMESON sick to C.C.S. 28 sick admitted during the past 24 hours and 12 wounded passed through A.D.S. W.R.M.	
	23	9pm.	Nothing special to report. CAPTAIN C.A. WEBSTER detailed for duty for relief of CAPTAIN JAMESON. CAPTAIN MCKAY RAMC TC reported for duty with the unit & taken on the strength accordingly. 20 sick admitted during past 24 hours & 6 wounded passed through. W.R.M.	
	24	9pm	Nothing special to note. Posts visited and working satisfactory. 35 Sick admitted to hospital and 18 wounded passed through A.D.S. W.R.M.	
	25	9pm.	Work carrying on and evacuations working smoothly. Soup Kitchens working well. Still a great percentage of sick from N Y D FEVER. 21 sick passed through and 11 wounded during past 24 hours. W.R.M.	
	26	9pm.	Nothing special to note. Captain McKAY detailed to relieve Captain C.A. WEBSTER. 18 sick admitted + 5 wounded passed through. W.R.M.	
	27.	9pm.	Nothing special. Visited posts + found all satisfactory. 35 Sick admitted to Hospital and 9 wounded passed through A.D.S. W.R.M.	

1875 Wt. W593/826 1,000,000 4/15 J.B.C. & A. A.D.S.S./Forms/C. 2118.

Instructions regarding War Diaries and Intelligence Summaries are contained in F. S. Regs., Part II. and the Staff Manual respectively. Title Pages will be prepared in manuscript.

WAR DIARY
or
~~INTELLIGENCE SUMMARY~~

(Erase heading not required.)

Army Form C. 2118

Place	Date 1917 June	Hour	Summary of Events and Information	Remarks and references to Appendices
RUYAULCOURT	28	9pm	Another series of cases of Gas Poisoning from Phosgene Gas admitted and passed through A.D.S. during the past 24 hours. The first batch were all very serious. Two died before reaching the A.D.S. One officer and 2 others died in spite of venesection being done and treatment carried as in the Appendix 3. The other cases improved after venesection had been done & were removed to C.C.S. 14 sick admitted to Hospital and 15 gassed & wounded passed through the A.D.S. during the past 24 hours. W.R.M.	App. 3
			Orders for handing over left of evacuation to 1/1st Field Ambulance app. 4.	
	29		During the past 24 hours, more cases of gassed cases have passed through the A.D.S. The cases appeared slight but grave symptoms supervened in some of them later & one died in the A.D.S. It is to be noted that the symptoms are delayed for 24 hours & then may be very severe and even fatal. Venesection was carried in certain of the slight cases but in all the severe it was done with hopeful results. It is also to be noted that the pulse in gassed cases seems to be good & full even up to very last phase and so different from the pulse in poisoning from Chlorine where the pulse is small & quick. 28 sick admitted during the past 24 hours and 83 wounded passed through the A.D.S. Transfer of the posts on the right section of evacuation completed satisfactorily. W.R.M.	

1875 Wt. W593/826 1,000,000 4/15 J.B.C. & A. A.D.S.S./Forms/C. 2118.

Instructions regarding War Diaries and Intelligence Summaries are contained in F. S. Regs., Part II. and the Staff Manual respectively. Title Pages will be prepared in manuscript.

WAR DIARY
or
~~INTELLIGENCE SUMMARY~~
(Erase heading not required.)

Army Form C. 2118

Place	Date 1917 June	Hour	Summary of Events and Information	Remarks and references to Appendices
RUYAULCOURT.	30	9pm.	More cases of gas passed through during the past 24 hours. There have been altogether 92 cases from enemy shells and of these 1 officer and five men have died. The rest of the cases are doing well. Some cases have come through gassed by our own shells but that is doubtful. The conclusion to be drawn from these cases is that any movement after gassing is fatal and that all cases should be bled as soon as possible if the cases indicate it. Venesection seems to be the treatment in severe cases along with morphine hypodermically + fresh air + no movement. The treatment carried out in the cases in appendix 4. 18 sick passed through the Hospital and 12 wounded or gassed passed through the ADS during the past 24 hours. W.R.M.	App. 4.
			During the month 792 patients were admitted into hospital and the greatest percentage were suffering from N.Y.D. FEVER.	
			During the month 366 wounded passed through the A.D.S.	
			During the month 419 cases of Scabies were treated by the Sulphur vapour method and of these only 26 came for a second treatment & 5 for a third.	
			The health of the unit is good + there is very little sickness.	
			W.R. Matthews. Lt Col. RAMC T.F. OC 1/2 East Lanc Fd Ambce 42nd Div.	

1875 Wt. W593/826 1,000,000 4/15 J.B.C. & A. A.D.S.S./Forms/C. 2118.

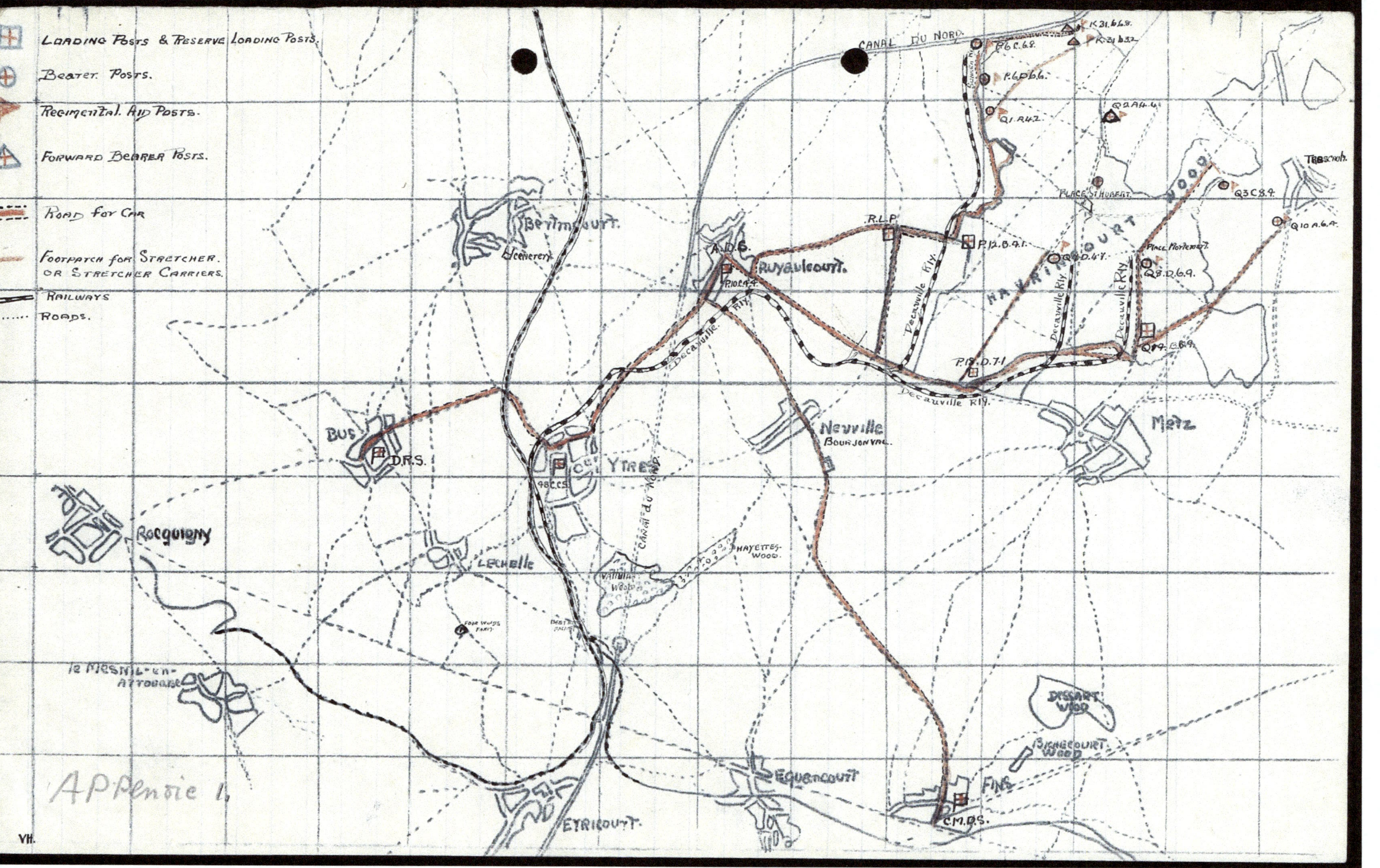

Loading Posts & Reserve Loading Posts.
Bearer Posts.
Regimental Aid Posts.
Forward Bearer Posts.
Road for Car
Footpath for Stretcher or Stretcher Carriers.
Railways
Roads.
Canal du Nord
Bertincourt.
Ruyaulcourt.
A.D.S.
R.L.P.
Decauville Rly.
Havrincourt Wood
Place St Hubert
Metz
Neuville Bourjonval.
Bus
D.R.S.
Ytres
48 C.C.S.
Rocquigny
Lechelle
Hayettes Wood.
Canal du Nord
le Mesnil-en-Arrouaise
Equancourt
Fins
C.M.D.S.
Etricourt.
Dessart Wood
Appendix 1.
VII.

OPERATION ORDERS NO 3 by
Lt. Col W.R. Matthews R.A.M.C.T.
O.C. 1/2nd. East Lancashire Field Ambulance.

Copy No 3.

Ref. Map 57c.

The datatchment of this unit now stationed at Camp Marley (Chuignolles) will move on Friday 8th. June by Route March in Two One Day Stages.

First Day from Camp Marley to Peronne . Second Day from Peronne to Ruyaulcourt.

Rations. The unexpended portion and one days rations to be carried.

DRESS. Marching Order with One Blanket and Great Coat Rolled on Pack. Steel Helmets to be worn. Box Respirators and P.H. Helmets to be carried.

Particular attention must be paid to March and Road discipline .

Two Motor Lurries will report to Camp Marley on Friday morning to convery surplus Blankets, Stretchers and Trestles.

Two G.S. Waggons and 1 Double Limber will report at Camp Marley on Wednesday night for conveying Section Equipment and Stores. On arrival at Peronne O.C. detatchment will report to Town Major, and enquire for Billetts for the night These will probably be the old Main Dressing Station.

All Patients to be evacuated by Wednesday and Hospital clear by Thursday morning. Cases not fit to return to units should be sent to Convalescent Camo

Signed. W.R.Matthews.
Lt. Col.R.A.M.C.T.

Copy No.1 O.C.Marley Camp Detachment.
2 File.
3 War Diary.
4-6-17

Appendix 2.

Copy No..2.....

Operation orders No 4 by

Lt. Col. W.R. Matthews R.A.M.C.T.

O.C. 1/2nd. East Lancashire Field Ambulance.

Reference Map 57c.

The Field Ambulance will evacuate from area to right of line K 32 d 8.0 - Q 2 c 8.0. - P 12 b 3.0. to Divisional Boundary.
Posts on the Left of that line will be handed over to 1/1st. East Lancashire Field Ambulance on 29th inst at 6.p.m.
" C " Section under Capt. Turner will take over the Advanced Dressing Station at Q 14 d 1.7.
The remainder of the personnel of " B " Section will remain at Mill Farm Relay Post P 18d7.1. to form Working Party for construction of Regimental Aid Post at Q 10 a 6.6 and Regimental Aid Post at Q 3 c 9.4.

Signed. W.R. Matthews. Lt. Col.R.A.M.C.T.

O.C. 1/2nd. East Lancashire Field Ambulance.

Copy No 1 File
" 2 War Dairy.

Appendix 3

Appendix 4

GAS POISONING.

GENERAL LINES OF TREATMENT ADOPTED.

3. (a) Disturbance of patient prevented and obviated as far as possible to prevent more of the poisonous gas entering the circulation.

(b) All clothing and equipment removed with as little disturbance to the patient as possible.

(c) $\frac{1}{4}$ gr Hypodermic injection of Morphine given.

(d) Ammonia capsules broken and applied by means of lint for inhalation taking care not to apply it too close to the nostrils so as not to produce coughing which aggravates the condition.

(e) Venesection performed in all but slight cases as early as possible and 14-16 ozs of blood removed, and until the blood loses its dark tarry colour and flows freely from the vein.

(f) Oxygen inhalation if indicated.

(g) Patients removed into the fresh air.

(h) Sips of mixture of hot milk and brandy by the mouth.

(i) Hot water bottles applied to sides and feet.

(j) Massage to cardiac area.

(k) Patient after venesection placed in a position with head and shoulders raised from stretcher.

W R Matthews.

30/6/17.

Lieutenant-Colonel,
Commanding 1/2nd E.Lancs Field Ambulance.

WO 95/2908

140/2208

CONFIDENTIAL.

WAR DIARY

OF

1/2nd EAST LANCASHIRE FIELD AMBULANCE.

FROM :- July 1st, 1917 TO :- July 31st, 1917.

(VOLUME VII)

9

July 1917

WAR DIARY
or
~~INTELLIGENCE SUMMARY~~
(Erase heading not required.)

Army Form C. 2118

Instructions regarding War Diaries and Intelligence Summaries are contained in F. S. Regs., Part II. and the Staff Manual respectively. Title Pages will be prepared in manuscript.

Place	Date 1917 July	Hour	Summary of Events and Information	Remarks and references to Appendices
RUYAULCOURT.	1	9pm.	Nothing special to note. Conference of Os C at A.D.M.S office reference the move of unit to new area; certain points suggested by A.D.M.S. to be carried out. 9 sick admitted to hospital and 1 wounded passed through during the past 24 hours. Unit expected to move within a week; no new works begun. W.R.M.	REF. MAP 67C P10 C.4.4. FRANCE 1/40000.
	2.	9pm.	Nothing special to note beyond visit of MAJOR GENERAL COMMANDING 42nd Division to thank unit for the work done in connection with the recent gas cases. Unit expected to move on the 6th. 16 sick admitted to hospital during the last 24 hours and one wounded. CAPTAIN C.A. WEBSTER left on 10 days leave to U.K. W.R.M.	57C N.E 57C S.E FRANCE 1/20,000
	3	9pm	Received notice that unit is to move on the 6th inst into new area. Had a visit from O.C. of incoming Field Ambulance. Five more cases of gas poisoning passed through the A.D.S. during the night. Two died, the others were slight. Venesection should be done in all cases whether the effects are slight or otherwise as slight cases become fatal in a very short time unless venesected early. 15 sick and nine wounded. W.R.M.	
		11.50	Orders received for unit to move from present Divisional area to new area. W.R.M.	
	4	9pm.	Conference of Os.C at A.D.M.S with reference to move to new Divisional area. Evacuation of right sector to be taken over by 1/1st EAST LANCS FD AMBCE, on 5th at 8 A.M. Advanced party of one officer + 2 O.R. to leave on 5th for new camp area by motor lorry. 12 sick admitted and 3 wounded passed through A.D.S. W.R.M.	

1875 Wt. W593/826 1,000,000 4/15 J.B.C. & A. A.D.S.S./Forms/C. 2118.

Instructions regarding War Diaries and Intelligence Summaries are contained in F. S. Regs., Part II. and the Staff Manual respectively. Title Pages will be prepared in manuscript.

WAR DIARY ~~or~~ ~~INTELLIGENCE SUMMARY~~

(Erase heading not required.)

Army Form C. 2118

Place	Date 1917 July	Hour	Summary of Events and Information	Remarks and references to Appendices
RUYAUL-COURT 57C. P10 C.4.4.	5.	9pm.	1 officer 2 O.R. left for new divisional area today. Evacuation of right sector of Divisional Area taken over by 1/1st Field Ambulance at 8 A.M. Section 'C' rejoined unit from forward Advanced Dressing Station. Orders issued for move of unit by route march along with 125th INF. BDE GROUP. appendix I. 8 sick admitted and 5 wounded passed through the ADVANCED DRESSING STATION. W.R.M.	REF SHEET 57C. P10 C.4.4 FRANCE 1/40,000.
GOMIE-COURT. 57C. A23 C8.2	6.	9pm.	Reached GOMICOURT: men marched well: picked up 5 O.R. from the BDE on the march: 2 O.R. detained with unit: camp site good one but no huts or buildings for hospital purposes: 12 C.S. obtained from TOWN MAJOR: arranging for the personnel less one T.S.D. to be in billets. 2 O.R. sick in hospital. W.R.M.	57c N.E. 57c S.E. FRANCE 1/20,000. SHEET 57c. 1/40000 FRANCE
	7.	9pm.	Getting camp ready and hospital for patients: expect to have two huts for the use of sick: general fatigue + routine. CAPTAIN McKAY reported for duty from 232 F.C. RE. W.R.M.	
	8.	9pm.	Camp fatigue + company drill: nothing special to note. W.RM.	
	9.	9pm.	Company drill for sections: special attention to getting fit again. W.RM.	
	10.	9pm.	General routine + hospital work: conference at A.D.M.S. with regard to the training: scheme of suggested training drawn up. Lt. SHARPIN for duty with 211th BDE R.F.A. Scheme of training see appendix 2. W.RM.	
	11.	9pm.	General routine of Training and Hospital duties; one hospital hut in the course of erection to hold sixteen patients. W.R.M.	

1875 Wt. W593/826 1,000,000 4/15 I.B.C. & A. A.D.S.S./Forms/C. 2118.

Army Form C. 2118

Instructions regarding War Diaries and Intelligence Summaries are contained in F. S. Regs., Part II. and the Staff Manual respectively. Title Pages will be prepared in manuscript.

WAR DIARY

~~INTELLIGENCE SUMMARY~~

(Erase heading not required.)

Place	Date 1917 July	Hour	Summary of Events and Information	Remarks and references to Appendices
GOMIECOURT 57C A23c 8.2.	12,	9pm.	Routine TRAINING and Hospital duties. Section o taking turns weekly in Hospital duties by TENT SUBDIVISION. Nothing special to note. CAPTAIN MACKAY detailed for duty as M.O. i/c D.T. + struck off strength. W.R.M.	REF SHEET 57C 1/40,000 FRANCE
	13,	9pm.	Routine: nothing special to note. W.R.M.	
	14.	9pm.	Routine training + hospital duties. CAPTAIN WEBSTER returned from leave. W.R.M.	
	15,	9pm.	Routine: nothing special to note. One hospital hut completed. W.R.M.	
	16,	9pm.	Routine training and Hospital duties. CAPTAIN TURNER on leave to U.K. for ten days: nothing special to note. W.R.M.	
	18.	9pm	Routine + Hospital duties; nothing special to note W.R.M.	
	20.	9pm.	Routine + Hospital duties: nothing special to note W.R.M.	
	21.	9pm.	Routine training + Hospital duties: men getting fit and very little sickness in the unit. T.A.B. inoculations being completed. W.R.M.	
	22	9pm	Routine training + Hospital duties: nothing special to note W.R.M.	
	23.	9pm.	Routine training + Hospital duties: nothing special to note. Inspection of A.S.C. TRANSPORT wagon by O.C. 42nd D.W. TRAIN. W.R.M.	

Instructions regarding War Diaries and Intelligence Summaries are contained in F. S. Regs., Part II. and the Staff Manual respectively. Title Pages will be prepared in manuscript.

WAR DIARY

or

~~INTELLIGENCE SUMMARY~~

(Erase heading not required.)

Army Form C. 2118

Place	Date 1917 July	Hour	Summary of Events and Information	Remarks and references to Appendices
GOMIECOURT. 57C A23 C8.2.	24	9pm.	Routine training & Hospital duties: nothing special to note. W.R.M.	REFSHEET 57C. 1/40000 FRANCE.
	25	9pm.	Routine training & Hospital duties: nothing special to note. Report on TRANSPORT by OC 42nd DIV. TRAIN. Exception taking to shoeing of horses otherwise report good. CAPTAIN PURNES RAMC T.F. and tent subdivision of B section left for duty at NO 3 C.C.S. GREVILLERS. LT. SHARPIN returned from duty with 211 BDE. R.F.A. W.R.M.	
	26	9pm.	Routine training and Hospital duties: nothing special to note. W.R.M.	
	27	9pm.	Routine training & Hospital duties: nothing special to note. W.R.M.	
	28	9pm.	Routine training & Hospital duties: nothing special to note. W.R.M.	
	29	9pm.	Routine training & Hospital duties. CAPTAIN TURNER returned from 10 days leave to U.K. CAPTAIN C.A. WEBSTER left for F.G.C.M. LT. SHARPIN detailed for duty with 4th ARMY DUNKIRK & struck off strength. W.R.M.	
	30	9pm.	Routine training & Hospital duties: nothing special to note. A/989 A.S.C. DR MULLINS J. sentenced to 21 days F.P. No1 & to forfeit 46 days pay. W.R.M.	
	31	9pm.	Routine training and Hospital duties; nothing special to note. W.R.M. During the month the health of the unit has been particularly good and the	

1875 Wt. W593/826 1,000,000 4/15 J.B.C. & A. A.D.S.S./Forms/C. 2118.

Instructions regarding War Diaries and Intelligence Summaries are contained in F. S. Regs., Part II. and the Staff Manual respectively. Title Pages will be prepared in manuscript.

WAR DIARY

or

~~INTELLIGENCE~~ SUMMARY

(Erase heading not required.)

Army Form C. 2118

Place	Date 1917 July	Hour	Summary of Events and Information	Remarks and references to Appendices
GOMIE-COURT	31	9pm	men are looking well and fit. Sports have been taken part in by the unit and certain amount of success has attended unit and especially in the football knock out competition where the team of the unit was in the final. This shows a good indication of the fitness of the men and officers. Very few cases of sickness during the month from the unit. No cases of infectious disease or venereal disease. The conduct of the men has been good no serious crime has been committed by any member of unit.	REF SHEET 57C 1/40,000.
			During the month 215 cases have been admitted into Hospital from the 125th BDE. + Brigade units giving a daily average of 6.93 admissions. Most of the admissions have been N.Y.D. FEVER (Ref. Appendix 3 + 4.)	Appendix 3+4
			During the month 478 patients were treated for SCABIES by the Sulpho-vapour treatment. Of these 365 were first admissions and the remainder 113 had a second or subsequent treatment on the next or following days. The treatment continues to be satisfactory and efficacious both for SCABIES and PEDICULOSIS. (Ref appendix 5 + 6).	Appendix 5+6
			W R Matthews Lt. Col. RAMC T.F. OC 1/2 East Lanc Fd. Amb. 42nd Div.	

1875 Wt. W593/826 1,000,000 4/15 I.B.C. & A. A.D.S.S./Forms/C. 2118.

appendix 1.

1/2nd. East Lancashire Field Ambulance Order No. 5 .

By Lt. Col. W.R. Matthews. R.A.M.C.T.

Map Ref. 57c. 1/40,000 5 - 7 - 17

The unit will move from RUYAULCOURT 57cP10c4.4. along with 125th. Inf. Brigade by Route March on the 6th. inst to GOMIECOURT 57cA23c8.2.

Reveille 3.a.m.

March off 6.a.m.

Cross Roads at BUS to be reached by 7.10.a.m.

Small party will be left behind to hand over to relieving Field Ambulance of 58th. Division.

Strict March Discipline must be maintained on March.

Signed. W.R.Matthews. Lt. Col R.A.M.C.T.
O.C. 1/2nd. East Lancashire Field Ambulance.

1 Copy War Dairy

1 Copy File

appendix II.

Scheme of Training

Time	Monday	Tuesday	Wednesday	Thursday	Friday	Saturday	Sunday
6-30 am. to 7-15 am	Physical Drill	Physical Drill	Physical Drill	Physical Drill	Physical Drill	Physical Drill	
9-0 am. to 10-15 a.m.	Squad Drill	Squad Drill	Company Drill	Squad Drill	Squad Drill	Company Drill	Church Parade
10-30 a.m. to 12-0	Company Drill	Company Drill	Stretcher Drill or Lecture	Company Drill	Company Drill	Stretcher Drill or Lecture	
2-0 pm. to 4-0 pm.	Lecture and Box Respirator Drill	Route March with Transport	Compulsory Sports.	Lecture and Box Respirator Drill	Route March with Transport	No Parade	

Appendix 3.

DAILY RATE OF SICK DURING THE MONTH OF JULY 1917.

1/2nd E.Lancs. Field Ambulance.

Date.	No.Admitted.		
1.	9		
2	16		
3	15		
4	12		
5	8		
6	-		
7	-		
8	7		
9	-		
10o	9		
11	4		
12	9		
13	-		
14	4		
15	7		
16	11		
17	7		
18	7		
19	8		
20	7		
21	7		
22	5		
23	7		
24v	4		
25	5		
26	9		
27	12		
28	2		
29	7		
30	17		
31	[illegible]	Total for Month	215.
		Daily average.	6 . 93.

Appendix 4

Sick & Wounded Chart. July 1917.

1/2nd E Lancs. Fd Ambulance.

20
15
10
5
1

MOVE
MOVE

1 2 3 4 5 6 7 8 9 10 11 12 13 14 15 16 17 18 19 20 21 22 23 24 25 26 27 28 29 30 31

Sick ——
Wounded ——

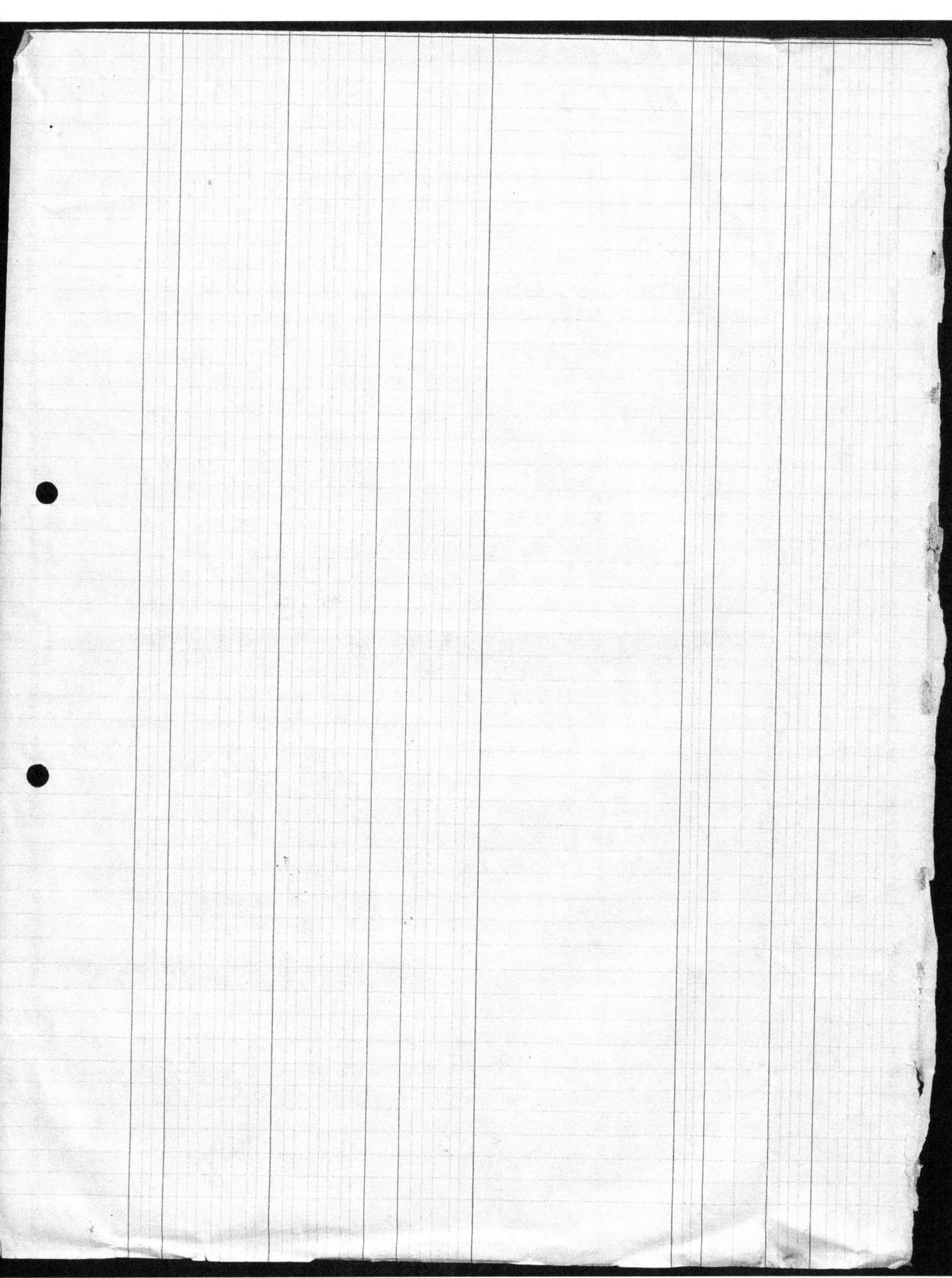

Summary of Scabies Patients treated month ending July 31st/17

Date	1st Bath	2nd Bath	3rd Bath	4th Bath	5th Bath	
July 1st	15	1	-	-	-	
" 2	19	2	1	-	-	
" 3	21	1	1	-	-	
" 4	23	1	-	1	-	
" 5	16	-	1	-	-	
" 9	5	1	1	-	-	
" 10	3	-	-	-	-	
" 11	3	-	-	-	-	
" 12	10	2	-	-	-	
" 13	16	5	-	-	-	
" 14	13	3	2	1	-	
" 15	11	4	-	1	-	
" 16	24	6	-	-	-	
" 17	14	6	2	-	1	
" 18	8	4	-	-	-	
" 19	13	3	1	2	-	
" 20	13	4	-	1	-	
" 21	13	4	2	-	-	
" 22	4	1	3	1	-	
" 23	16	6	2	1	1	
" 24	12	3	2	1	-	
" 25	16	-	3	3	-	
" 26	14	3	-	-	-	
" 27	9	-	1	-	2	
" 28	15	4	1	1	-	
" 29	10	3	-	1	-	
" 30	9	1	1	-	-	
" 31	20	2	-	1	-	
TOTALS	365	70	24	15	4	

Grand Total 478 Patients

Average = 17 Patients per day

Appendix 5.

July 31st 1917.

W. E. Cooper.
L/Cpl.

Appendix 6.

Scabies Chart for July 1917.
1/2nd E Lancs. Fd Amb. CE.

30
25
20
15
10
5
1

Move

1 2 3 4 5 6 7 8 9 10 11 12 13 14 15 16 17 18 19 20 21 22 23 24 25 26 27 28 29 30 31

CONFIDENTIAL

WAR DIARY

OF

1/2nd (EAST LANCASHIRE) FIELD AMBULANCE.

FROM :- 1st August, 1917. TO :- 31st August, 1917.

(VOLUME VIII)

Instructions regarding War Diaries and Intelligence Summaries are contained in F. S. Regs., Part II. and the Staff Manual respectively. Title Pages will be prepared in manuscript.

WAR DIARY

~~or~~

~~INTELLIGENCE SUMMARY~~

(Erase heading not required.)

Army Form C. 2118

Place	Date 1917 Aug	Hour	Summary of Events and Information	Remarks and references to Appendices
GOMIE-COURT. 57C A23 C8.2.	1.	9pm.	Routine training and Hospital duties; officers and N.C.O.s of unit attended course of lectures on Anti-Gas ~~[illegible]~~ precautions and appliances at the DIV. GAS School. nothing else special to note. W.R.M.	REFSHEET 57C. 1/40,000 FRANCE.
	2.	9pm	Routine training consisting of lectures in billets: weather too wet for field work. Hospital duties as usual: nothing else special to note of importance. W.R.M.	
	3.	9pm.	Routine training as far as the weather allowed; instruction in the principles + application of anti-gas appliances. CAPTAIN HUMMEL sick to C.R.S. Certain amount of what appears to be malaria about. W.R.M.	
	4.	9pm.	Routine training and Hospital duties as usual. nothing special to note. Acting A.D.M.S from today for A.D.M.S. 42nd Divn on leave. W.R.M.	
	5.	9pm.	nothing special to note. Church Parades. visited A.D.M.S. Office. medically examined rejects by M.O. of units of recent drafts. W.R.M.	
	6.	9pm.	Nothing special to note. Routine training and Hospital duties being carried on. visited A.D.M.S office. W.R.M.	

1875 Wt. W593/826 1,000,000 4/15 J.B.C. & A. A.D.S.S./Forms/C. 2118.

Instructions regarding War Diaries and Intelligence Summaries are contained in F. S. Regs., Part II. and the Staff Manual respectively. Title Pages will be prepared in manuscript.

WAR DIARY

~~or~~

~~INTELLIGENCE SUMMARY~~

(Erase heading not required.)

Army Form C. 2118

Place	Date 1917 Aug	Hour	Summary of Events and Information	Remarks and references to Appendices
GOMIE-COURT 57c A23 C8.2.	7.	9pm.	Routine training and Hospital duties: visited A.D.M.S. office to day, nothing special to note. W.R.M.	REF SHEET 57C. 1/40,000 FRANCE
	8	9pm.	Routine training & hospital duties as usual. Divisional R.A.M.C. Sports held this afternoon. very successful. G.O.C. Division presented prizes. visited A.D.M.S.'s Office. nothing special to note. W.R.M.	
	9.	9pm.	Routine training & hospital duties. particular attention has been given to day with regard to the using of the BOX RESPIRATOR: men having been drilled & carrying stretchers with patients for an hour on end with the Box Respirator on. visited A.D.M.S.'s office. nothing special to note. W.R.M.	
	10	9pm.	Routine training and hospital duties; route march of sections: inspection of transport: horses harness & vehicles in good condition: visited A.D.M.S. Office. nothing special to note. W.R.M.	
	11.	9pm.	Routine training and Hospital duties: visited A.D.M.S.'s office: nothing special to note. W.R.M.	
	12	9pm.	Church Parades and Hospital duties: visited A.D.M.S.'s Office: nothing to note. W.R.M.	

1875 Wt. W593/826 1,000,000 4/15 J.B.C. & A. A.D.S.S./Forms/C. 2118.

Army Form C. 2118

Instructions regarding War Diaries and Intelligence Summaries are contained in F. S. Regs., Part II. and the Staff Manual respectively. Title Pages will be prepared in manuscript.

WAR DIARY

or

~~INTELLIGENCE SUMMARY~~

(Erase heading not required.)

Place	Date 1917 Aug.	Hour	Summary of Events and Information	Remarks and references to Appendices
GOMIE-COURT 57C A23 C8.2	13	9pm.	Routine training and Hospital duties: visited A.D.M.S. Office. Examined rejects from new drafts as to fitness for frontline duties W.R.M.	REF. SHEET 57C. 1/40,000 FRANCE
	14.	9pm	Routine training and Hospital duties: parade for route march in full marching order: transport paraded and inspected: horses & harness in good condition: visited A.D.M.S. office: nothing special to note W.R.M.	
	15.	9pm.	Routine training & Hospital duties: visited A.D.M.S. Office: nothing special to note: visit by D.D.M.S. VI Corps: inspected SCABIES Box treatment apparatus & pleased with the results: treated 62 cases today and 53 yesterday. W.R.M.	
	16.	9pm.	Routine training & hospital duties: anti gas precautions & wearing of Box Respirator for one hour during training. visited A.D.M.S. Office: nothing special to note: criticisms from D.D.M.S. visit. W.R.M.	
	17	9pm	Routine training & hospital duties: route march: visited A.D.M.S. office & handed over duties to A.D.M.S. on his return from leave: nothing to note W.R.M.	
	18.	9pm.	Routine training & hospital duties. Received warning notice from BDE that entraining begins on the 22nd inst. W.R.M.	

Instructions regarding War Diaries and Intelligence Summaries are contained in F. S. Regs., Part II. and the Staff Manual respectively. Title Pages will be prepared in manuscript.

WAR DIARY

~~or~~

~~INTELLIGENCE SUMMARY~~

(Erase heading not required.)

Army Form C. 2118

Place	Date 1917 Aug	Hour	Summary of Events and Information	Remarks and references to Appendices
GOMIE-COURT	19	9pm.	Church Parades & Hospital duties: orders received for unit to march by route march with 125th BDE to new area; CAPTAIN PURVES + tent subdivision of B section rejoined unit less one other rank sick in hospital. CAPTAIN STEWARD + 2 OR detailed to proceed by rail as advance party to new area Ref. Appendix I. W.R.M.	REF SHEET 57C 1/40000 FRANCE.
BOUZIN-COURT.	20	9pm.	Field Ambulance arrived: accommodation in billets: men marched well no one falling out 15 OR from BDE units picked up on the march: move by rail to new area expected in a few days: preparations accordingly. W.R.M.	Appendix I.
	21	9pm.	Nothing special to note: preparations made in anticipation of move. Men fit and well. W.R.M.	
	22	9pm.	Field Ambulance to move by rail tomorrow: one section less transport by one train CAPTAIN PURVES + B Section detailed: remainder of Field Ambulance and TRANSPORT by another train: motor ambulances by road in convoy. Ref Appendix II	Appendix II.
27 4 19b 3.6.	23	9pm	In troop train en route for new area. Sheet 27 4 19b 3.6. W.R.M.	REF SHEET 27 + 28 1/40000 FRANCE + BELGIUM
	24	9pm.	Reached camping ground in new area at 3.30 AM. accommodation in tents men marched well and fit. W.R.M.	
	25	9pm.	Field to move by route march to RED FARM Sheet 28 G 5 d 9.5 and prepare a CORPS MAIN DRESSING STATION. Ref. Appendix III W.R.M.	Appendix III

1875 Wt. W593/826 1,000,000 4/15 J.B.C. & A. A.D.S.S./Forms/C. 2118.

Army Form C. 2118

Instructions regarding War Diaries and Intelligence Summaries are contained in F. S. Regs., Part II. and the Staff Manual respectively. Title Pages will be prepared in manuscript.

WAR DIARY
~~or~~
~~INTELLIGENCE~~ SUMMARY
(Erase heading not required.)

Place	Date 1917 AUG	Hour	Summary of Events and Information	Remarks and references to Appendices
RED FARM 28G5d9.5	26.	9pm.	Arrived at RED FARM and preparing CORPS MAIN DRESSING STATION: visit of D.D.M.S. XIX CORPS. W.R.M.	Ref SHEET 28 1/40000 FRANCE + BELGIUM
	27.	9pm.	Preparations proceeding for opening of Dressing station. Sick from units being seen & being admitted. Dressing station consists of two main wards and [illegible] which at present are for personnel. Extensive cleaning of site needed [illegible] W.R.M.	
	28	9pm.	Active preparations proceeding satisfactorily: visit of D.D.M.S. XIX CORPS. Certain instructions received & carried out. W.R.M.	
	29	9pm.	Preparations practically completed & CORPS MAIN DRESSING STATION ready for reception of wounded & sick. Orders received for 1 Officer & 2 Bearer Sub Divisions to go up to the front & be under O.C. 1/1st Field AMBCE. W.R.M.	
	30	9pm.	CORPS MAIN DRESSING STATION receiving from [illegible] today: detailed CAPTAIN W TURNER + 2 Bearer Subdivisions to proceed to YPRES tomorrow & report to O.C. 1/1 EAST LANC. FD AMBCE. Ref Appendix IV. W.R.M.	Appendix IV
	31	9pm.	TWO BEARER SUBDIVISIONS under CAPTAIN TURNER left for A.D.S YPRES today at 3 p.m: wounded being brought in numbers all during the last 24 hours: nothing special to note; arrangements working satisfactorily. W.R.M.	

1875 Wt. W593/826 1,000,000 4/15 J.B.C. & A. A.D.S.S./Forms/C. 2118.

Instructions regarding War Diaries and Intelligence Summaries are contained in F. S. Regs., Part II. and the Staff Manual respectively. Title Pages will be prepared in manuscript.

WAR DIARY
or
~~INTELLIGENCE~~ SUMMARY

(Erase heading not required.)

Army Form C. 2118

Place	Date. 1917 AUG	Hour	Summary of Events and Information	Remarks and references to Appendices
RED FARM 28G5d9.5	31	9pm.	During [illegible] to 19 Aug 445 cases had treatment for Scabies by the STEAM sulphur bath. There was a daily average approximately of 23 patients and of these about 6 percent had to come more than twice and these visits were more for other skin conditions. Attached is the sick rate of the affiliated brigade which was below the average for the Bgde. appendix V The health of the unit has been good during the month. There has been no infectious or [illegible] disease amongst the unit & the men are fit & well. W. R. Matthews. Lt. Col. RAMC T.F. O.C. 1/2 East Lanc Fd Amb 42nd Div.	REF. SHEET 28 1/40000 FRANCE + BELGIUM appendix V

Appendix I

Orders by Lieut.-Colonel.W.R.Matthews.R.A.M.C.T.F.
O.C.1/2nd.E.Lancs. Field Ambulance.

August 19th 1917.

Reference Maps. LENS. 1/100,000 and 57.C. 1/40,000.

---

1. The Field Ambulance will move to-morrow the 20th inst by road to BOUZINCOURT area as under :-
Route ACHIET LE PETIT - MIRAUMONT - BEAUCOURT - MESNIL - MARTINSART - BOUZINCOURT.
Starting point level crossing A 28 b 0.2.
Fall in 9-30.a.m. Move off 9-45.a.m.
To be at starting point 10-19.a.m.
2. There will be a halt of 1 hour for Dinner at 12 noon.
3. Dress. Full marching order. Steel helmets will be worn.
4. Reveille 5.a.m. Fall in 5-30.a.m. Camp Fatigue 5-30 to 7.a.m. Breakfast 7-30.a.m.
5. All waggons to be loaded by and ready to move off by 9-30.a.m.
6. 1 Officer and 2 Other Ranks as advance party.
7. N.C.O's in charge of sections will be held responsible that packs and haversacks are properly packed and contain nothing but what they should contain.
Water Bottles to be filled by 8-30.a.m.
Motor Ambulances will move by road according to instructions.

(sd) W.R.Matthews.
Lt-Colonel.R.A.M.C.T.F.
O.C.1/2nd.E Lancs. Field Ambulance.

Appendix II

Orders by Lieut.-Colonel W.R.Matthews.R.A.M.C.T.F.

O.C.1/2nd.E.Lancs. Field Ambulance.

August 22nd 1917.

MOVE. "B" Section will move by No.6 Train at 5-21.a.m. tomorrow 23rd inst. Hot Meal will be served at 12 midnight.

Fall in 1.a.m. March off 1-15.a.m..

The remainder of the Field Ambulance and Transport will proceed by No.8 Train at 1-16.p.m. on the 23rd inst.

Fall in 9.a.m. March off 9-15.a.m.

Dress. Marching order water bottles filled.

Unexpended portion of the days rations will be carried on the man. Steel Helmets will be worn. Packs to be properly packed and nothing to be in the haversack except the knife fork , spoon and rations (Including iron rations.)

All cooking utensils and baggage to be loaded on wagons by 8-30.a.m.

The Motor Ambulance and Cycle left behind will report to O.C 1/1st E.Lancs. Field Ambulance at Beaucourt sur Ancre Station at 2.p.m. on the 23rd inst. 3 days rations to be carried.

(sd) W.R.Matthews.
Lt-Col.R.A.M.C.T.F.
O.C.1/2nd.E.Lancs. Field Ambulance.

Appendix III

Orders by Lieut.-Colonel W.R.Matthews.R.A.M.C.T.F.

O.C.1/2nd.E.Lancs. Field Ambulance.

August 24th 1917.

Reference Maps Belgium & France 1/40,000

Sheets 27 and 28.

MOVE. The Field Ambulance will move to-morrow the 25th inst. by March Route from Sheet 27 L.19.b.3.6. to Red Farm Sheet 28.G.5.d.9.5. and prepare a Corps Main Dressing Station.

Reveille 5.a.m. Fall in 5-30.a.m. Breakfast 7.a.m.

Fall in 8-45.a.m. March off 9.a.m.

Dress. Marching Order, Steel Helmets to be worn.

(sd(W.R.Matthews.
Lt-Col.R.A.M.C.T.F.
O.C.1/2nd.E.Lancs. Field Ambulance.

Appendix IV

Orders by Lieut.-Colonel W.R.Matthews,R.A.M.C.T.F.

O.C.1/2nd.E.Lancs. Field Ambulance.

August 30th 1917.

Reference Maps Belgium & France,

1/40,000 Sheets 27 & 28.

MOVE. Two Bearer sub Divisions at full strength (less 1 Officer and Transport) will proceed by road on the afternoon of the 31st inst. to the Prison YPRES, and on arrival will come under the orders of the O.C.1/1st E.Lancs. Field Ambulance. These two Bearer Sub Divisions will be rationed by the 1/2nd.E.Lancs. Field Ambulance until 2nd September inclusive. Captain Turner and B. & C. Bearer Sub Divisions will proceed as above.

Fall in 2-15.p.m. Move off 2-30.p.m.

(sd) W.R.Matthews.
Lt-Colonel.R.A.M.C.T.F.
O.C. 1/2nd.E.Lancs. Field Ambulance.

Appendix
V

Sick August 1917.

60
50
40
30
20
15
10
5
1

1 2 3 4 5 6 7 8 9 10 11 12 13 14 15 16 17 18 19 20 21 22 23 24 25 26 27 28 29 30 31

CONFIDENTIAL.

WAR DIARY
of
O.C.,1/2nd East Lancs.Field Ambulance.

From 1st September 1917 to 30th September 1917.

(VOLUME IX)

Instructions regarding War Diaries and Intelligence Summaries are contained in F. S. Regs., Part II. and the Staff Manual respectively. Title Pages will be prepared in manuscript.

WAR DIARY
or
INTELLIGENCE SUMMARY
(Erase heading not required.)

Army Form C. 2118

Place	Date 1917 Sept	Hour	Summary of Events and Information	Remarks and references to Appendices
RED FARM 28G5d95	6	9pm	Wounded coming in from all units; more than half of the wounded to day are gassed cases; gas evidently lachrimatory in character & mustard in consistence: arrangements for receiving & evacuation of wounded working well. Visited by D.D.M.S. XIX CORPS & also by A.D.M.S. 42nd Division; 5 P.B. MEN reported for duty as Batmen. W.R.M.	REF SHEET 28 1/40,000 FRANCE & BELGIUM
	7	9pm.	Wounded still coming in; wounds are chiefly shell wounds; CAPTAIN TURNER relieved by CAPTAIN BURNES for duty with the bearer subdivisions. W.R.M	
	8	9pm.	Fewer wounded during the last 12 hours. 7 O.R. for reinforcements to day. CAPTAIN STEWARD reported again for duty with unit. W.R.M.	
	9.	10pm.	Visit from D.D.M.S. Vth Corps re certain arrangements to be carried out in the C.M.D.S.; CAPTAIN STEWARD & CAPTAIN JACOB ordered to proceed to ENGLAND as reinforcements. W.R.M.	
	10.	11.30.	Nothing special to note; wounded & gassed cases coming in in a steady stream. The gassed cases all have been "Mustard gas". One orderly killed at the A.D.S. W.R.M.	
	11.	11.15	Nothing special to note; most of wounded coming in are gassed cases and they are chiefly affected by lachrymatory gas. W.R.M.	

1875 Wt. W593/826 1,000,000 4/15 J.B.C. & A. A.D.S.S./Forms/C. 2118.

Instructions regarding War Diaries and Intelligence Summaries are contained in F. S. Regs., Part II. and the Staff Manual respectively. Title Pages will be prepared in manuscript.

WAR DIARY

~~or~~

~~INTELLIGENCE~~ SUMMARY

(Erase heading not required.)

Army Form C. 2118

Place	Date	Hour	Summary of Events and Information	Remarks and references to Appendices
RED FARM 28G5d9.5	1917 Sept. 1.	9pm.	Nothing special to note: Wounded have been coming in a continuous stream the past 24 hours: wounds nearly all shell wounds. W.R.M.	REF SHEET 28 1/40000 FRANCE + BELGIUM
	2.	9pm.	Nothing special to report: visit from A.D.M.S 47th Division: Quite satisfied with arrangements made for sick + wounded: suggested the erecting of a gas reception hut or tent for treatment of gas cases: also the improvement of the horse standings. W.R.M.	
	3.	9pm	Nothing special to note: patients have been coming in a steady stream all night + today: arrangements made for sick of units around to be seen at BRANDHOEK. CAPTAIN STEWARD detailed for duty with 32 C.C.S. W.R.M.	
	4.	9pm.	Wounded coming in regularly + amongst them have been a number of gassed cases: venesection been done on some of them. W.R.M.	
	5	9pm.	Gassed cases in numbers today: mustard gas: symptoms chiefly are nausea conjunctivitis of eyes, erythema + blistering of skin especially on parts where the skin perspires more than in other places. Secret orders for a shunt tomorrow morning + preparations accordingly made. CAPTAIN S. JACOB reported for duty. W.R.M.	

1875 Wt. W593/826 1,000,000 4/15 J.B.C. & A. A.D.S.S./Forms/C. 2118.

Instructions regarding War Diaries and Intelligence Summaries are contained in F. S. Regs., Part II. and the Staff Manual respectively. Title Pages will be prepared in manuscript.

WAR DIARY

~~or~~

~~INTELLIGENCE~~ SUMMARY

(Erase heading not required.)

Army Form C. 2118

Place	Date 1917 SEP.	Hour	Summary of Events and Information	Remarks and references to Appendices
RED FARM 28 [illegible] 5 d 9.5	12	9pm.	Had 15 lethal shell gas cases today. Venesection [illegible] and injected one oz of saline solution of Hexamine 24 grs to the ounce subcutaneously. The effect and relief given is most marked and the dyspnoea & cardiac distress disappears. Morphia 1/4 grain is also given and half [illegible] of Oxygen [illegible] by inhaler. All the cases improved & sent off to C.C.S. with orders that all cases are to be treated likewise. W.R.M.	REF. SHEET 28 1/40000 FRANCE + BELGIUM
	13.	11pm.	Nothing special to report. Less wounded & gassed have come in today and the gassed cases are chiefly lachrymatory. W.R.M.	
	14	11.30pm	Nothing special to report: instructions received to hand over to incoming F.A. tomorrow and await further orders. CAPTAIN GOLDING W.R.M. RAMC T.C. detailed for duty with	
	15.	11.30pm	Handed over C.M.D.S. to 2/1 WESSEX FIELD AMBULANCE. W.R.M.	
	16	9pm.	Received orders for unit to move into new area with 126th BDE on the 19th. W.R.M.	
	17	9pm	Nothing special to note: preparations prior to move being made: all the bearer subdivisions rejoined unit today from the advanced posts. W.R.M.	

1875 Wt. W593/826 1,000,000 4/15 J.B.C. & A. A.D.S.S./Forms/C. 2118.

Instructions regarding War Diaries and Intelligence Summaries are contained in F. S. Regs., Part II. and the Staff Manual respectively. Title Pages will be prepared in manuscript.

WAR DIARY

or

~~INTELLIGENCE SUMMARY~~

(Erase heading not required.)

Army Form C. 2118

Place	Date 1917 SEP	Hour	Summary of Events and Information	Remarks and references to Appendices
RED FARM 28G5d9.5	18	10pm.	Received orders to move alongwith 126 Inf. BDE on 19th: issued orders to that effect. Detailed CAPTAIN TURNER to go with advance party to new area for billetting. W.R.M.	REF SHEET 28 1/40000 FRANCE + BELGIUM
WINNEZELE AREA.	19	9pm.	Arrived at WINNEZELE AREA. Billets intended for unit still occupied and so had to go to other billets: men accommodated in three big barns and comfortable. Received orders to move to new billets in WINNEZELE tomorrow. Issued orders for that purpose. W.R.M.	REF SHEET 27+28 1/40000 BELGIUM + FRANCE.
	20	9pm.	Orders to move with 126th BRIGADE GROUP from WINNEZELE AREA to WORM-HUDT AREA by route march. Detailed CAPTAIN WEBSTER + two orderlies as advance billetting party. W.R.M.	APPENDIX 1, 2, 3.
WORM-HUDT. AREA.	21	9pm.	Reached WORMHUDT area. Men marched well and complimented by Brigadier on their marching. Men accommodated in three barns, comfortable. Orders received to move by route march from WORMHUDT area to TETEGHEM. by route march. CAPTAIN WEBSTER detailed with 2 O.R. to go as advance party for billetting. W.R.M.	

1875 Wt. W593/826 1,000,000 4/15 J.B.C. & A. A.D.S.S./Forms/C. 2118.

Instructions regarding War Diaries and Intelligence Summaries are contained in F. S. Regs., Part II. and the Staff Manual respectively. Title Pages will be prepared in manuscript.

WAR DIARY

or

~~INTELLIGENCE~~ SUMMARY

(Erase heading not required.)

Army Form C. 2118

Place	Date 1917 SEP.	Hour	Summary of Events and Information	Remarks and references to Appendices
TETEGHEM	22	10pm.	Arrived at TETEGHEM AREA. men marched well. Billetted in the Ferme du Nord. Orders received to move to LA PANNE tomorrow. CAPTAIN WEBSTER detailed to proceed as advance party for billeting: no casualties. W.R.M.	REF. SHEET. SHEET 19 + 27. 1/40000
LA PANNE	23	9pm.	Arrived at LA PANNE + men in comfortable billets: no casualties on the march. W.R.M.	SHEET FURNES 1/40000.
	24	9pm.	Orders received from ADMS to take over the A.D.S. at OOSTDUNKERE and at OOSTDUNKERKE BAINS + NIEUPORT BAINS from ambulances of 66th Divn. Taking over to be completed by 10 AM tomorrow. Detailed CAPTAIN TURNER to conduct "C" SECTION to proceed tonight to OOSTDUNKERE BAINS + remain there for tonight. CAPTAIN WEBSTER ordered to conduct "C" SECTION to NIEUPORT BAINS tomorrow at 6 AM. "B" SECTION under CAPTAIN PURNES to proceed to A.D.S. at OOSTDUNKERKE + "A" SECTION to proceed to A.D.S. OOSTDUNKERKE BAINS. W.R.M.	SHEETS COXYDE + LOMBARTZYDE. APPENDIX 4 + 5.
OOST DUNKERKE BAINS	25	9pm.	H.Q. Section arrived at OOSTDUNKERKE BAINS and took over A.D.S. from ambulance of 66th DIVISION. "B" SECTION arrived at OOSTDUNKERKE and took over the A.D.S. there. "C" SECTION arrived at NIEUPORT BAINS and took over the A.D.S. there. no casualties + move completed by 10. A.M. W.R.M.	

1875 Wt. W593/826 1,000,000 4/15 J.B.C. & A. A.D.S.S./Forms/C. 2118.

Instructions regarding War Diaries and Intelligence Summaries are contained in F. S. Regs., Part II. and the Staff Manual respectively. Title Pages will be prepared in manuscript.

WAR DIARY
or
INTELLIGENCE SUMMARY
(Erase heading not required.)

Army Form C. 2118

Place	Date 1917 SEPT.	Hour	Summary of Events and Information	Remarks and references to Appendices
OOST DUNKERKE BAINS	26	9pm.	Went and saw the ADS. at OOST DUNKERKE & NIEUPORT BAINS and made arrangements for evacuation of the line. Found all satisfactory. W.R.M.	REF. SHEET FURNES 1/40,000 COXYDE + LOMBART-ZYDE. 1/20,000.
	27	9pm.	Nothing special to note: evacuation of sick & wounded working smoothly. Enemy shelled heavily during the night. W.R.M.	
	28	9pm.	Visited ADS. at NIEUPORT BAINS + OOST DUNKERKE & found all satisfactory. W.R.M.	
	29	9pm.	Nothing special to note. Enemy shelling & aerial activity heavy. W.R.M.	APPENDIX 6.
	30	9pm.	Visited ADS. & found all satisfactory. W.R.M.	
			Health of the unit during the month good. Marching ~~march~~ powers of the unit very good and no casualties during the route marches extending over six days. No cases of diarrhoea or infectious disease reported. Two casualties in the unit from shelling, PTE HODGKINSON + PTE W. L. ANSON. Both buried at BRANDHOEK. SERGT. HORNE of this unit awarded the military medal.	
			W.R. Matthews. Lt.Col RAMC T.F. O.C. 1/2 EAST LANC FD. AMBCE. 42nd Div.	

1875 Wt. W593/826 1,000,000 4/15 J.B.C. & A. A.D.S.S./Forms/C. 2118.

Copy No. 2.. APPENDIX 1.

Movement Order No 6.

By Lt. Col. W.R.Matthews. R. A. M. C. T. F.

O.C. 1/2nd. East Lancashire Field Ambulance.

Ref. Sheets 27 & 28 1/40.000 18 - 9 - 17.

1.		Field Ambulance will move with 126th. Infantry Brigade to-morrow 19th. inst from BRANDHOEK area to WINNEZEELEarea No 1.
2.	Route.	By switch Road north of Poperinghe Road Junction L.4.b.8.2. WATOU & DROGLANDT. Unit will pass starting point at 7.18 a.
3.	Dress.	Marching Order. Steel Helmets, P.H.Helmet and Box Respirators will be worn. Service Cap will be strapped to velise.
4.	March Discipline	Strict March Discipline to be maintained One Officer will march in front of unit two Officers will march in rear. Field Ambulance will march as one Coy. Distance of 300 yds betweent units to be kept.
5.	Advance Party.	Capt. W. Turner and Two Mounted Orderlies will meet Staff Capt at cross roads G.5.d.0.2. After being shown billetting area this party will mett unit at road junction J.12.b.8.7.

Signed. W.R. Matthews.
Lt. Col.R.A.M.C.T.F.

O.C. 1/2nd. East Lancs.Field Ambulance.

Copy No 1. File.
" " 2 War Diary.

"20th. sept.

Reveille 5. moved off in morning to new ground at other side of Winnezeele.

Copy No. 2. APPENDIX 2.

Movement Order No 7.
By Lt. Col. W.R.Matthews. R. A. M. C. T. F.
O.C. 1/2nd. East Lancashire Field Ambulance.

20th. Sept. 1917.

Ref. Sheet 27 1/40.000

1. Move. Unit will move with 126th. Infantry Brigade Group from the WINNEZEELE area No 1 to WORMHOUDT area on the 21st. inst.

2. Reveille. Reveille 5.30. a.m.
Parade 6.a.m.
March off 10 a.m.

3. Route. Route will be via Cross Roads J.21.b.2.6. to WORMHOUDT.
Unit will pass starting point at 10.19.a.m.

4. March Discipline. Strict March Discipline will be maintained The usual hourly halts will be observed.

5. Dress. Marching Order. P.H.Helmets. Box Respirators. and Steel Helmets will be worn.

6. Transport. All Transport will march under the orders of 126th. Brigade Transport Officer.
Units Transport will pass the starting point at 9.30.a.m.
Gaps of 200 yds will be left between Transport of units and a gap of 20 yds between each group of 6 vehicles.

7. Advance Party. Capt W.Turner and two Mounted orderlies will meet Staff Capt at Area Commandants office WORMHOUDT at 8.a.m.

Signed. W.R.Matthews.
Lt. Col. R.A.M.C.T.F.

O.C. 1/2nd. E.Lancs. Field Ambulance.

Copy No 1 File
" " 2 Dairy.

1a

Copy No. 2.

APPENDIX 3.

Movement Order No 8.
By Lt. Col.W.R.Matthews. R.A.M.C.T.F.
O.C. 1/2nd. East Lancashire Field Ambulance.

Reference Sheets 19 & 27 1/40.000 — 21st. Sept.1917

1.	Move.	Unit will move with 126th. Infantry Brigad Group to-morrow 22nd. inst to TETEGHEM area.
2.	Reveille.	Reveille 5.30.a.m. Parade 6.a.m. March off 10.15.a.m.
3.	Route .	WILDER-LES-CHEMINS cross roads 0.17.d.19.2 . GAJ GHOEK. Unit will pass starting point at 10.18.a.m.
4.	March Discipline.	Strict March Discipline will be maintained The usual hourly halts will be observed.
5.	Dress.	Marching Order.Steel Helmets. Box Respirators and P.H. Helmets will be worn.
6.	Transport.	Transport will march under orders of 126th. Infantry Brigade Transport Officer Starting point Road Junction C.11.b.6.7.
7.	Advance Party	Capt Turner and two mounted orderlies will meet Staff Capt at Area Commandants office at 8.a.m.

Signed. W.R. Matthews.
Lt. Col.R.A.M.C.T.F.

O.C. 1/2nd. East Lancashire Field Ambulance.

Copy No 1. File.
" 2. Dairy.

Copy No.2.. APPENDIX 4.

Movement Order No 9.
By Lt. Col.W.R.Matthews. R. A. M. C. T. F
O.C. 1/2nd. East Lancashire Field Ambulance.

22 - 9 - 17.

Ref.Sheets 27 1/40.000.FURNES 1/40.000.1/20.000.Coxyde and Lombartzyde.

1. Move.	Unit will move with 126th. Infantry Brigade Group from the TETEGHEM area to"La Panne" on 23rd. inst.
2. Reveille.	Reveille 4. a.m. Parade 4.30 a.m. March Off. 6.p.m.
3. March Discipline	Strict March discipline will be maintained. Usual hourly halts will be observed.
4. Dress.	Marching Order. Steel Helmets.Box Respirators and P.H. Helmets will be worn.
5. Advance Party	Capt. C.A.Webster and two mounted orderlies will proceed to LA PANNE at 5.a.m. to meet Staff Capt and arrange for Billetts.

Signed. W.R. Matthews.
Lt. Col.R.A.M.C.T.F.

O.C. 1/2nd. East Lancashire Field Amb.

Copy No 1 File.
" 2 Dairy.

Copy No.1..

Movement Order No 9.
By Lt. Col.W.R.Matthews. R. A. M. C. T. F
O.C. 1/2nd. East Lancashire Field Ambulance.
22 - 9 - 17.

Ref.Sheets 27 1/40.000.FURNES 1/40.000.1/20.000.Coxyde and Oombartzyde.

1. Move. Unit will move with 126th. Infantry Brigade Group from the TETEGHEM area to"La Fanne" on 23rd. inst.

2. Reveille.
Reveille 4. a.m.
Parade 4.30 a.m.
March Off. 5.a.m.

3. March Discipline Strict March discipline will be maintained.
Usual hourly halts will be observed.

4. Dress. Marohing Order.
Steel Helmets.Box Respirators and P.H. Helmets will be worn.

5. Advance Party Capt. C.A.Webster and two mounted orderlies will proceed to LA FANNE at 5.a.m. to meet Staff Capt and arrange for Billetts.

Signed. W.R. Matthews.
Lt. Col.R.A.M.C.T.F.

O.C. 1/2nd. East Lancashire Field Amb.

Copy No 1 File.
" 2 Dairy.

APPENDIX 5.

Copy No..2...

Movement Order No. 10
By Lt. Col.W.R.Matthews. R.A.M.C.T.F.
O.C. 1/2nd. East Lancashire Field Ambulance.

Reference Maps FURNES 1/40.000. Provisional Issue.
1/20.000 COXYDE and LOMBARTZYDE. Sheets.

24 Set. 1917.

1. Move "C" Section. "C" Section will March out at 3.p.m. 24th. inst and proceed to OOST DUNKERKE BAINS under the command of Capt. W. Turner R.A.M.C.T.F. and 1st. Lt. A.M. Dickinson U.S.M.S. They will remain at OOST DUNKERKE BAINS overnight and proceed to Nieuport Bains Advanced Dressing Station at 6.a.m. 25th. inst under the command of Capt. C.A. Webster R.A.M.C.T. Capt. W.Turner returning to Headquarters of Field Amb at LA PANNE after conducting section to OOST DUNKERKE BAINS on 24th. inst.

2. Move "A" & "B" Sections.

Reveille	4.a.m.
Breakfast	5.a.m.
Fall in	5.45.a.m.
March Off	6.a.m.

3. March Discipline. Strict March Discipline will be maintained Steel Helmets, Box Respirators and P.H. Helmets will be worn. Field Amb. will march in column of Sections

4. Rations. Rations will be carried in Bulk. Waterbottles will be filled.

5. Destinations. "B" Section under Capt. Purves will detatch itself from "A" Section at junction of OOST DUNKERKE & OOST DUNKERKE BAINS Roads and proceed to OOST DUNKERKE Advanced Dressing Station.
"A" Section under Capt. Turner will proceed to Main Dressing Station OOST DUNKERKE BAINS
Move to be completed by 10 a.m.

Signed. W.R.Matthews.
Lt. Col.R.A.M.C.T.F.

O.C. 1/2nd. E.Lancs. Field Ambulance.

Copy No 1 File.
" 2.Dairy.

Sick September 1917.

APPENDIX 6

CONFIDENTIAL.

WAR DIARY

of

O.C., 1/2nd East Lancashire Field Ambulance.

1st October 1917 to 31st October 1917.

VOLUME 10.

Instructions regarding War Diaries and Intelligence Summaries are contained in F. S. Regs., Part II. and the Staff Manual respectively. Title pages will be prepared in manuscript.

WAR DIARY
or
INTELLIGENCE SUMMARY.
(Erase heading not required.)

Army Form C. 2118.

Place	Date 1917 Oct.	Hour	Summary of Events and Information	Remarks and references to Appendices
OOST DUN-KERKE BAINS.	1.	9pm	Visit of A.D.M.S. 42nd Divn & went round part of line: nothing special to note. W.R.M.	REF SHEET FURNES 1/40000 COXYDE + LOMBART-ZYDE 1/20,000.
	2.	9pm	Lt Col W. R. MATTHEWS left on leave. CAPTAIN W. J. PURNES in command. LAITER-IE ROYAL POST visited also NIEUPORT BAINS visited and found all satisfactory accommodation for 100 sitting + 100 lying cases. gas arrangements very good. W.R.M.	
	3	9pm	Visit & inspection by Surg. Gen. O'KEEFE D.M.S. 4th ARMY and by A.D.M.S. 42nd Division. of H.Q. of Field Ambulance and then visited the A.D.S. at NIEUPORT BAINS. Both seemed pleased with all arrangements. CAPT. G ALSTER U.S.M.S. detailed for duty with 1/8 MANCHESTER REGT. W.R.M.	
	4	9pm	Visited A.D.S. NIEUPORT BAINS and LAITERIE ROYAL. Visited also the A.D.S. at OOST DUNKERQUE. Received orders from A.D.M.S. to hand over to an ambulance of 41st Division relief to be completed by the 6th inst. On relief the unit will relieve the 91st Field Ambulance in the line at the NIEUPORT SECTOR with H.Q. of Field Ambulance at X13 b 5.0. Relief to be completed by the 7th inst. A.D.S. to be at NIEUPORT. W.R.M.	

A7092 Wt. W1259/M1293 750,000. 1/17. D. D & L. Ltd. Forms/C2118/14.

Instructions regarding War Diaries and Intelligence Summaries are contained in F. S. Regs., Part II. and the Staff Manual respectively. Title pages will be prepared in manuscript.

WAR DIARY

~~or~~

~~INTELLIGENCE SUMMARY.~~

(*Erase heading not required.*)

Army Form C. 2118.

Place	Date 1917 Oct.	Hour	Summary of Events and Information	Remarks and references to Appendices
OOSTDUNKERKE BAINS	5	9pm	Movement order to O.C. 'B' Section that on relief by FD AMBCE of 41st Division 'B' Section would relieve a section of the 91st FD AMBCE in the line of the NIEUPORT SECTOR with A.D.S. at M34 a5.4. and 6 R.A.P. + one artillery post. See Appendix I W.R.M.	REF APP. I
	6.	9pm	Visited ADS at NIEUPORT with O.C. 91st Field Ambulance, visited also the CAB STAND with accommodation for 4 DAIMLERS + 1 FORD. Wounded taken from CAB STAND + A.D.S. to C.M.D.S. to OOSTHOEK. A.D.S. at NIEUPORT has accommodation for 150 cases and 50 gassed cases in elephant huts separate from A.D.S. H.Q. at OOSTDUNKERKE relieved by the 138 Fd. Ambce. W.R.M.	
X13.6.50	7	9pm	Arrived at X13.6.5.0 with A + C Sections + relieved the personnel of the 91st FD. AMBCE took over hospital there. W.R.M	REF MAP. FURNES 1/40,000 PROV. ISS.
	8	9pm	Visited A.D.S. NIEUPORT with D.A.D.M.S. 42nd DIV. went round the line. Work at H.Q. chiefly fatigues. W.R.M.	
	9	9pm	CAPTAIN WEBSTER detailed to take over A.D.S. Gas arrangements improved. Fatigue work at COXYDE for erection of elephant huts. W.R.M.	

A7092 Wt. W128 9/M1293 750,000. 1/17. D. D & I. Ltd. Forms/C2118/14.

Army Form C. 2118.

Instructions regarding War Diaries and Intelligence Summaries are contained in F. S. Regs., Part II. and the Staff Manual respectively. Title pages will be prepared in manuscript.

WAR DIARY
~~or~~
~~INTELLIGENCE SUMMARY.~~
(*Erase heading not required.*)

Place	Date 1917 Oct.	Hour	Summary of Events and Information	Remarks and references to Appendices
X13.6.5.0	10	9pm.	Visit from ADMS. TRANSPORT LINES moved to GROOTKWINTE FARM. Fatigue work being carried on for erection of elephant huts. W.R.M.	
	11	9pm.	Conference at ADMS. office concerning trench foot treatment centres. W.R.M.	
	12	9pm.	Visited ADS. NIEUPORT. Soup kitchens established on right half sector. ADMS. inspected H.Q. + GROOTKWINTE FARM. CAPTAIN NEAME RAMC T.C. taken on the strength but attached to 36 C.C.S. W.R.M.	
	13.	9pm.	TRANSPORT moved to GROOTKWINTE FARM + a bathing party of 1 NCO and 10 OR. detailed as a bathing party at C.M.D.S. W.R.M.	
	14	9pm.	Visited ADS. NIEUPORT. Soup kitchens established and working. Fatigue work being carried at COXYDE with the erection of elephant huts and also in roof repairing at GROOTKWINTE FARM. Lt Col MATTHEWS returned from leave at 1/3R command. Lt Col J M LOWE rejoined unit from L. of C. W.R.M.	REF. MAP. FURNES 1/40,000 Prov. Is.
	15	9pm.	Inspection of H.Q. arrangements, elephant huts + transport lines at GROOTKWINTE FARM. W.R.M.	
	16	9pm.	Routine duties. Fatigues being carried on satisfactorily. W.R.M.	

A7092 Wt. W128.9/M1293 750,000. 1/17. D. D & I. Ltd. Forms/C2118/14.

Army Form C. 2118.

Instructions regarding War Diaries and Intelligence Summaries are contained in F. S. Regs., Part II. and the Staff Manual respectively. Title pages will be prepared in manuscript.

WAR DIARY
or
INTELLIGENCE SUMMARY.

(*Erase heading not required.*)

Place	Date Oct 1917	Hour	Summary of Events and Information	Remarks and references to Appendices
X13 b.5.0	17	9pm	visited ADS. NIEUPORT with ADMS. + DADMS. Certain improvements to be carried out in the ADS. for patients & personnel. visited posts on the left sector. Found everything satisfactory. Gas arrangements good. W.R.M.	
	18.	9pm	Routine and fatigue work at COXYDE and GROOTKWINTE FARM. Erection of shelters for personnel proceeding satisfactorily. W.R.M.	
	19.	9pm	visited ADS. & found arrangements satisfactory and rearrangement of the accommodation being carried out. Soup kitchens working well. Visited the CABSTAND. More protection for patients required & also for personnel. W.R.M.	
	20.	9pm	Routine work and fatigues being carried out satisfactorily. One elephant hut erected. W.R.M.	
	21	9pm	Routine work & fatigues. Inspection of Transport lines. W.R.M.	
	22	9pm	Routine work & fatigues. CAPTAIN H.C. GALSTER struck off strength. W.R.M.	
	23.	9pm	Routine work & fatigues. Visit to ADS. NIEUPORT. W.R.M.	
	24	9pm	Routine work & fatigues. ADS. work & POSTS satisfactory. W.R.M.	

A7092 Wt. W128 9/M1293 750,000. 1/17. D. D & I. Ltd. Forms/C2118/14.

Instructions regarding War Diaries and Intelligence Summaries are contained in F. S. Regs., Part II. and the Staff Manual respectively. Title pages will be prepared in manuscript.

WAR DIARY

or

~~INTELLIGENCE~~ SUMMARY.

(*Erase heading not required.*)

Army Form C. 2118.

Place	Date 1917 Oct.	Hour	Summary of Events and Information	Remarks and references to Appendices
X13.b.5.0	25	9pm.	G.O.C. 42nd DIVISION + A.D.M.S. visited A.D.S. NIEUPORT + REDAN POST + Soup Kitchen on left sector + found every thing satisfactory. W.R.M.	
	26.	9pm.	Routine duties and fatigues: nothing special to note. W.R.M.	
	27	9pm.	Orders received to hand over A.D.S. at NIEUPORT and B.P. and H.Q. at COXYDE to 1/3 EAST LANC FD AMBCE on the 30/31st Oct. and 31st Oct. + 1st November, relief to be completed by 6 AM 1 NOV. 1917. Visited A.D.S. and GROOT KWINTE FARM. Found all satisfactory. W.RM.	
	28	9pm.	Issued orders for move to camp of 1/3rd Field AMBCE and for the relief of the A.D.S. + B.P. + CAB STAND. See appendix II. W.RM.	
	29	9pm.	Routine and fatigues carried on and all work being continued + completed before transfer if possible. W.RM.	
	30	9pm.	Routine work + fatigues. Reliefs for B.P. being carried out tonight. CAPTAIN R.T. HERDMAN RAMC T.C. taken on strength of unit. W.RM	

A7092 Wt. W128.9/M1293 750,000. 1/17. D. D & I. Ltd. Forms/C2118/14.

Army Form C. 2118.

WAR DIARY
or
~~INTELLIGENCE SUMMARY.~~

(*Erase heading not required.*)

Instructions regarding War Diaries and Intelligence Summaries are contained in F. S. Regs., Part II. and the Staff Manual respectively. Title pages will be prepared in manuscript.

Place	Date 1917 Oct.	Hour	Summary of Events and Information	Remarks and references to Appendices
X13 G.5.0	31	9pm.	Half of relief of posts in NIEUPORT SECTOR completed and the other half completed to night and the relief of A.D.S. Part of baggage has been transferred to new camp. The completion of relief completed tomorrow.	
			The health of unit during the past month has been very good. There have been no cases of Trench FEET. Two casualties of slight character during the month but both remained with the unit.	
			The highest number of sick admitted during 24 hours was 30. The highest number of wounded admitted to the A.D.S. in 24 hours was 26. There have been a few cases of TRENCH FEET from the units of the DIVISION in the line. No cases of infectious disease admitted and the cases of diarrhoea have yielded to treatment.	REF APP III + IV.
			The unit is up to strength but 2 officers under strength.	
			W R Matthews. Lt. Col. RAMC T.F. OC 1/3 East Lancs Fd. Ambce 42nd Divn.	

MOVEMENT ORDER NO 11. Copy No....
By Capt. W.J.Purves.R.A.M.C.T.F.
For O.C. 1/2nd. East Lancashire Field Ambulance.

Map Ref. 1/40.000 FURNES.Provisional Issue. 4 - 10 - 17.

" B " SECTION.

"B"section at present stationed at A.D.S. OOST DUNKERKE will be relieved by an Ambulance of the 41st. Division on the 5th. & 6th inst. relief to be completed by 6.p.m. on the 6th. inst.

Arrangements will be made to accomodate "B" sec. in Cellars near at hand after 6.p.m.6th. inst.

On morning of 7th. "B"sec.will relieve the 91st.Field Ambulance 32 Divn. in the line of the NIEUPORT SECTOR with Headquarters of the Field Ambulance at COXYDE.
Relief to be completed by 10 a.m. 7th. inst.

" C " SECTION.

"C" section will be relieved by an Ambulance of the 41st. Division on the 5th. & 6th. inst. relief to be completed by 6.p.m. 6th. inst.
All personnel on being relieved will return to Headquarters at OOST DUNKERKE BAINS

A & C SECTIONS.OOST DUNKERKE BAINS

On morning of 7th.inst A & C sections will take over Headquarters of 91st. Field Amb. at COXYDE relief to be completed by 10 a.m.
On arrival at COXYDE the relief for the personnel of " B " section will commence immediately,
All parties going by Motor Ambulance to the A.D.S. NIEUPORT.
4Daimlers & 1 Ford will stand at CABSTAND X 6.a.2.8. to work between A.D.S.NIEUPORT and Hqrs. COXYDE & C.M.D.S. OOST HOEK.

Signed. W.J.Purves.Capt. R.A.M.C.T.F.

For O.C. 1/2nd. E.Lancs. Field Amb.

1. Copy War Dairy.
1. " File.

Appen. I

Movement Order No 12.
By Lt. Col W.R.Matthews.R. A. M. C. T. F.
O.C. 1/2nd. East Lancashire Field Ambulance.

Maps
Furnes. 1/40.000 Provisional Issue
Special Maps No 4 & 5 1/10.000

28 - 10 - 17.

<u>MOVE.</u>	The 1/3rd. East Lancs. Field Amb. will relieve this unit from the NIEUPORT sector of the line on the nights of 30th./31st.Oct. & 31st Oct./1st.Nov. This unit will take over the Camp of the 1/3rd.E.L.Field Ambulance at X.7.c.8.7.
Reliefs.	By arrangement with the O.C. 1/3rd.E.L.F.A. part of the relief will be made on the night of 29th./30th.inst. and the remainder of the reliefs for the Bearer Posts and Advanced Dressing Station will be effected on nights of 30/31st. inst and 31st.Oct & 1st.Nov. all moves to be completed by 6.a.m. 1st.Nov.
Personnel.	Men from the Bearer Posts and A.D.S. as soon as relieved will be detailed to report at Hqrs.Coxyde and remain there until further orders
Equipment.	All Equipment to be packed on Wagons ready to move on 30th./31st. inst.
Transport	Transport section will remain at DE GROOTE KWINTE FARM until further orders.
Stores.	All stores and equipment that do not belong to this unit will be handed over to incoming unit.

Signed. W.R.Matthews.Lt.Col.R.A.M.C.T.F.

O.C. 1/2nd.E.Lancs.Field Ambulance.

Copy No 1. O C. A.D.S.
" 2. War Dairy
" 3 File.

APP. II.

APP-EN-DIX. III

1/2ND
EAST LANCASHIRE
FIELD AMBULANCE.
No.
Date

SICK.

OCTOBER 1917.

Appendix IV

Sick & Wounded treated at A.D.S. October 1917

Sick —

Wounded —

WO95/2910

140/2578

W A R D I A R Y

OF

1/2nd EAST LANCASHIRE FIELD AMBULANCE.

FROM :- 1st November, 1917 TO :- 30th November, 1917.

(VOLUME XI)

23

Nov. 1917

Instructions regarding War Diaries and Intelligence Summaries are contained in F. S. Regs., Part II. and the Staff Manual respectively. Title pages will be prepared in manuscript.

WAR DIARY or INTELLIGENCE SUMMARY.

(*Erase heading not required.*)

Army Form C. 2118.

Place	Date 1917 NOV	Hour	Summary of Events and Information	Remarks and references to Appendices
X 7 C 8.7.	1	9pm.	Moved to new camping ground completed. Personnel in elephant hut shelters and patients in wooden huts. Horse standings & shelters want completion. Certain arrangements requiring revising especially as to accommodation for patients. CAPTAIN HERDMAN detailed for duty with DIV. A.C. D.D.M.S. XV Corps + A.D.M.S 42nd DIV. inspected GROOTKWINTEFARM. W.R.M.	REF SHEET FURNES 1/40000 PROV. ISSUE
	2	9pm.	Nothing special to report. Fatigue duties carried out with regard to the completion of Horse lines and elephant hut shelters. S.M. BLAND left the unit to be Lt. + QT. to 58th Field AMBULANCE W.R.M.	
	3.	9pm.	Fatigues continued and work being carried on. Conference at A.D.M.S. of Field Ambulance Commanders. W.R.M.	
	4.	9pm.	Work proceeding well. Stables progressing quickly towards completion. Beacon MEDICAL Board on men reported unfit for service at the front. W.R.M.	
	5	9pm.	Construction work & rebuilding hutments proceeding. Visited with D.A.D.M.S, the proposed centres for TRENCH FEET TREATMENT. made arrangements for commencement. LT. DICKENSON U.S.M.S. detailed as M.O. i/c 1/8 L.F. + proceeded to join unit & struck off strength accordingly. W.R.M.	

A7092 Wt. W128 9/M1293 750,000. 1/17. D. D & L. Ltd. Forms/C2118/14.

Instructions regarding War Diaries and Intelligence Summaries are contained in F. S. Regs., Part II. and the Staff Manual respectively. Title pages will be prepared in manuscript.

WAR DIARY

~~or~~

~~INTELLIGENCE SUMMARY.~~

(Erase heading not required.)

Army Form C. 2118.

Place	Date 1917 NOV	Hour	Summary of Events and Information	Remarks and references to Appendices
X7c8.7	6.	9pm	Construction work on stables + hutments proceeding satisfactorily. nothing special to note. W.R.M.	REF. SHEET FURNES 1/40,000
	7.	9pm.	Work proceeding well. STABLES expected to be occupied by tomorrow: nothing special to note. W.R.M.	
	8.	9pm.	Work on Stables so far complete so as to enable horses to get in. TRANSPORT moved from GROOTKWINTE FARM to new Stables in Camp at 2pm today. move reported completed by 4 p.m. W.R.M.	
	9	9pm.	Work on stables being continued. Routine work in Hospital. Nothing special to report. W.R.M.	
	10.	9pm.	Nothing special to note. Work proceeding satisfactorily. W.R.M.	
	11	9pm	Conference at A.D.M.S. office re move from this area. Details as to handing in Stores. CAPTAIN GIBSON detailed for duty with the 1/10 MANCHESTER REGT. MEDICAL BOARD held today. W.R.M.	

A7092 Wt. W125 9/M1293 750,000. 1/17. D. D & I. Ltd. Forms/C2118/14.

Army Form C. 2118.

Instructions regarding War Diaries and Intelligence Summaries are contained in F. S. Regs., Part II. and the Staff Manual respectively. Title pages will be prepared in manuscript.

WAR DIARY
~~or~~
~~INTELLIGENCE SUMMARY.~~

(Erase heading not required.)

Place	Date 1917 NOV	Hour	Summary of Events and Information	Remarks and references to Appendices
X7C8.7	12	9pm	LIEUT HALE USAMC taken on the strength and detailed for duty with 1/8 LANC FUSILEERS as O i/c MC. CAPTAIN HERDMAN left unit on termination of Contract.	REF SHEET FURNES 1/40,000
	13	9pm.	Nothing special to note. Handing over of stores being carried out in anticipation of move. CAPTAIN GIBSON returned to unit from doing duty with 1/10 MAN. REGT as O i/c MC. W.R.M	
	14	9pm.	Nothing special to note. Continuation of handing over of A.O. & R E Stores previous to moving out. W.R.M.	
	15	9pm.	Orders received for 1 section of the Field Ambulance to move with & under orders of the 127th Bde group on the 16th inst. Detailed "C" section to move to-morrow with 127th Bde group. Rest of unit to move with & under orders of 126th Inf. BDE on the 18th inst. W.R.M.	
	16	9pm.	"C" Section in charge of CAPTAIN WEBSTER and with CAPTAIN GIBSON left by route march for new area. TRANSPORT of section along with 127th BDE Transport. Orders received for rest of unit to move on 18th inst with 126th INF. BDE Group. W.R.M.	Appendix I

A7092 Wt. W128_9/M1293 750,000. 1/17. D. D & L. Ltd. Forms/C2118/14.

Instructions regarding War Diaries and Intelligence Summaries are contained in F. S. Regs., Part II. and the Staff Manual respectively. Title pages will be prepared in manuscript.

WAR DIARY
or
~~INTELLIGENCE~~ SUMMARY.

(Erase heading not required.)

Army Form C. 2118.

Place	Date 1917 NOV	Hour	Summary of Events and Information	Remarks and references to Appendices
X7C8.7.	17	9pm.	Conference at A.D.M.S's office with reference to move. Orders issued for the move of rest of unit to SYNTHE AREA tomorrow the 18th. Personnel to move by lorries + TRANSPORT by road. CAPTAIN PURVES arrived from leave to U.K. Awaiting orders for hour of move + details. W.R.M. A+B" Sections to move alongwith 126th BDE Group.	REF SHEET FURNES 1/40,000 appendix II
	18	9pm.	Unit arrived at the SYNTHE AREA and are billetted in St POL SURMER. Orders received for unit to march to WORMHUDT AREA A alongwith 126th BDE. GROUP. Detailed Ambulances to march in rear of column. W.R.M.	REF SHEET 27 1/40000.
WORMHUDT	19	9pm.	Arrived at WORMHUDT ARAEA. No casualties. Orders received to march to WORMHUDT AREA B alongwith 126th BDE Group. W.R.M.	
	20	9pm	Arrived at WORMHUDT AREA B. No casualties. Billetted in two farms. Orders received to move to WALLON CAPPEL area. W.R.M.	
	21	9pm.	Arrived at WALLON CAPPEL AREA + billetted in a farm. No casualties on the march. Orders to move to AIRE AREA. W.R.M.	REF SHEET HAZEBROUCK 5A.

A7092 Wt. W128 9/M1293 750,000. 1/17. D. D & L. Ltd. Forms/C2118/14.

Army Form C. 2118.

WAR DIARY

or

~~INTELLIGENCE~~ SUMMARY.

(Erase heading not required.)

Instructions regarding War Diaries and Intelligence Summaries are contained in F. S. Regs., Part II. and the Staff Manual respectively. Title pages will be prepared in manuscript.

Place	Date 1917 MAY	Hour	Summary of Events and Information	Remarks and references to Appendices
COEHM.	22	9pm.	Arrived at COEHM in the AIRE AREA. No casualties. No orders to move tomorrow. Unit billeted in farms. Men fit. W.R.M.	REFSHEET HAZEBROUCK 5A.
	23	9pm.	NIL to report. W.R.M.	
	24	9pm.	NIL to report. W.R.M.	
	25	9pm.	Orders received for one section to move to THIENNES tomorrow. Detailed 'B' section under CAPTAIN PURVES to move. W.R.M.	
	26	9pm	B section arrived at THIENNES + is looking after + evacuating sick for 125th BDE. while on the march on the 27th. Detailed 2 horse ambulances + 1 M.A.C. Cars for that purpose. 126th BDE moving from WITTES AREA to BERGUES AREA. Detailed Horse ambulance to follow up part of this Brigade. Orders received for the Field Ambulance to concentrate + march to MERVILLE on the 28th. W.R.M.	Appendix III

A7092 Wt. W128/9/M1293 750,000. 1/17. D. D & L. Ltd. Forms/C2118/14.

Instructions regarding War Diaries and Intelligence Summaries are contained in F. S. Regs., Part II. and the Staff Manual respectively. Title pages will be prepared in manuscript.

WAR DIARY

~~or~~

~~INTELLIGENCE SUMMARY.~~

(*Erase heading not required.*)

Army Form C. 2118.

Place	Date 1917 Nov	Hour	Summary of Events and Information	Remarks and references to Appendices
COEHM	27	9pm.	Advance party sent to MERVILLE of two Officers + 20 O.R. to take over the XV Corps R.S. Corps C.S. + Officers Rest Station. W.R.M.	OEF SHEET HAZEBROUCK 5A.
MERVILLE	28	9pm.	Arrived at MERVILLE by route march. Took over from 76th Field Ambulance the C.R.S. C.S.S. + O.R.S. Found the place very unsuitable in every way for C.R.S. no room for expansion very insanitary and in every way to be condemned. Officers Rest Station is good but needs improvements. C.S.S. suitable for the purpose in certain ways but better to be in huts. Horse standings good but no wagon lines. W.R.M.	
	29	9pm.	Still more convinced of unsuitability of place for C.R.S. many improvements needed to make the place in future passable. W.R.M.	
	30	9pm.	Visit of Corps Commander + D.D.M.S. of XV Corps. Condemned the place at once. Certain strictures passed about the place and the personnel. W.R.M. Health of unit good during last month + there has been no prevailing disease. Marching of men good. W.R. Matthews Lt Col RAMC T.F. O.C. 1/2 East Lanc Fd Ambce	

A7092. Wt. W128.9/M1293. 750,000. 1/17. D. D & L. Ltd. Forms/C2118/14.

App II

1/2nd. East Lancashire Field Ambulance Order No12
-0-0-0-0-0-0-0-0-0-0-0-0-0-0-0-0-0-0-0-0-0-0-0-0-0-0-0-0-0-0-0-0-

By Lt. Col W.R.Matthews.R.A.M.C.T.F.
O.C. 1/2nd. East Lancashire Field Ambulance.

Ref.Map 11. 1/20.000 Belgium 15.11.17

"C" section wi th Transport and Equipment complete will move to new area on the 16th. inst. under the orders of 127th. Infantry Brigade.

Fall in 8.15.a.m.

March off 8.30.a.m.

1 N.C.O. will be detailed to meet Staff Capt . at Leffrinckou cke to arrange for Billetts of section.

Dress. Marching Order.Steel Helmets.Box Respirators and P.H. Helmets.Water Bottles full and uncomsumed portion of days Ration in Haversack.

Strict attention to be paid to Road and March Discipline.

W.R. Matthews.
Lt. Col.R.A.M.C.T.F.
O.C. 1/2nd. East Lancas. Field Ambulance.

App II

1/2nd. East Lancashire Field Ambulance Order No 13

-o-o-o-o-o-o-o-o-o-o-o-o-o-o-o-o-o-o-o-o-o-o-o-o-o-o-o-o-o-o-o-o-o-o-

By Lieut Col W.R.Matthews.R.A.M.C.T.F.
O.C. 1/2nd. East Lancashire Field Ambulance.

Ref.Map 11. 1/20.000 Belgium. 17.11.17

The Field Ambulance (less One section) will move from present area to Synthe Area on 19th. inst.(per Motor Buses from Coxyde)

Fall in 8.a.m.

March off 8.30.a.m.

Dress. Marching Order.Steel Helmets.Box Respirators and P.H. Helmets.Water Bottles full and unconsumed portion of days Rations to be carried in Haversacks.

Transport A.S.C. H.T. will move by Road separate from the R.A.M.C. personnell under the orders of Transport Officer 126th. Brigade Group.

Motor Ambulances will proceed as a Motor Convoy under the orders of the C.O.

Cooks.Lt. Qmr .J.M.Lowe with the Cooks and Cooking utensils will proceed in advance by Motor Ambulance to Synthe Area.

W.R. Matthews.
Lt. Col R A.M.C.T.F.

O.C. 1/2nd. East Lancashire Field Ambulance.

app. III

1/2nd. East Lancashire Field Ambulance Order No 14

-o-o-o-o-o-o-o-o-o-o-o-o-o-o-o-o-o-o-o-o-o-o-o-o-o-o-o-o-o-o-o-

By Lt. Col W.R.Matthews.R.A.M.C.T.F.
O.C. 1/2nd. East Lancashire Field Ambulance.

Ref.Map 36a. 1/40.000 25.11.17

"B" section will move from Cohem to Thiennes to-morrow 26th. inst under Capt. W.J.PurvesR.A.M.C.T.F. Dress Marching Order, steel Helmets Box Respirators and P.H. Helmets. Water Bottles filled.
Unexpended portion of days rations to be carried in Haversack.
Lt.Qmr J.M.Lowe with One N.C.O. & One Man will proceed in advance to arrange for Billetts.

W.R.Matthews.
Lt. Col.R.A.M.C.T.F.

O.C. 1/2nd. East Lancashire Field Ambulance.

W A R D I A R Y

OF

1/2nd EAST LANCASHIRE FIELD AMBULANCE.

FROM :- December 1st, 1917 TO :- December 31st, 1917.

(VOLUME XII)

Army Form C. 2118.

WAR DIARY

~~or~~

~~INTELLIGENCE SUMMARY.~~

(Erase heading not required.)

Instructions regarding War Diaries and Intelligence Summaries are contained in F. S. Regs., Part II. and the Staff Manual respectively. Title pages will be prepared in manuscript.

Place	Date 1917 DEC	Hour	Summary of Events and Information	Remarks and references to Appendices
MERVILLE	1.	9pm.	Visited all places today found things going on satisfactory but after a lot to be done to get the place in any way shipshape. HAD a visit from the DDMS & Corps Staff Officer with regard to the place and especially the O.R.S. Report from DDMS about the place. W.R.M.	REF SHEET HAZEBROUCK 5A.
	2.	9pm.	"B" Section of the Field Ambulance under CAPTAIN PURNES detailed to relieve 75th Field Ambulance at the ECOLE CATORNE in BETHUNE. W.R.M.	REF SHEET BETHUNE Combined Sheet 1/40,000.
	3.	9pm.	Nothing special to report. Ordered to evacuate all patients from XV CORPS REST STATION to 54 C.C.S. 51 C.C.S. & to M.D.S. ECOLE CATORNE by D.D.M.S. XV. CORPS. W.R.M.	
	4.	9pm.	All patients evacuated from C.R.S. CORPS Officers Rest Station & CORPS Skin depot still being carried on under difficulties. Neither place at all suitable for the purpose. Ordered to move H.Q. Field Ambulance to the COLLEGE DES JEUNES FILLES, BETHUNE. W.R.M.	
BETHUNE COLLEGE des JEUNES FILLES.	5	9pm.	Headquarters of Field Ambulance moved to COLLEGE des Jeunes Filles, BETHUNE. Detachments still at Corps Officers Rest Station & Corps Skin depot MERVILLE. W.R.M.	

Army Form C. 2118.

WAR DIARY

or

~~INTELLIGENCE SUMMARY.~~

(Erase heading not required.)

Instructions regarding War Diaries and Intelligence Summaries are contained in F. S. Regs., Part II. and the Staff Manual respectively. Title pages will be prepared in manuscript.

Place	Date 1917 DEC.	Hour	Summary of Events and Information	Remarks and references to Appendices
COLLEGE des JEUNNES FILLES. BETHUNE	6	9pm.	Nothing special to report. Work being carried on both at Rest Station and Skin Depot. Much dissatisfaction over both places but every effort being made to improve them both although not very amenable to being so. W.R.M.	REF Gun medsheet BETHUNE 1/40000
	7.	9pm.	A.D.M.S inspected M.D.S at ECOLE CATORIVE. W.R.M.	
	8.	9pm.	Nothing special to note. Usual routine being carried out by all sections of Field Ambulance at BETHUNE + MERVILLE. W.R.M.	
	9	10pm.	Nothing special to note. W.R.M.	
	10	9pm.	Nothing special to note. W.R.M.	
	11.	10pm.	Visited site of No18 C.C.S with a view to forming a Divisional Rest Station at LAPUGNOY (D21a.2.7) with A.D.M.S. W.R.M.	1/2 FD AMB OP ORD NO 14 appendix 1
	12	9pm.	Received orders to detach a section to form D.R.S. at LAPUGNOY. Detailed "B" section to proceed tomorrow for that purpose therefore for sick. W.R.M.	
	13	9pm.	"B" section left for LAPUGNOY to form D.R.S. Reached there at 2.15pm. Is very ready to receive patients tomorrow at 10.A.M. W.R.M.	

Instructions regarding War Diaries and Intelligence Summaries are contained in F. S. Regs., Part II. and the Staff Manual respectively. Title pages will be prepared in manuscript.

WAR DIARY

or

~~INTELLIGENCE~~ SUMMARY.

(*Erase heading not required.*)

Army Form C. 2118.

Place	Date 1917 Dec.	Hour	Summary of Events and Information	Remarks and references to Appendices
COLLEGE des JEUNNES FILLES. BETHUNE	14	9pm.	Visited D.R.S. and found everything well prepared for patients. Visited ECOLE CATORIVE & found everything satisfactory. W. R. M.	REF MAP Combined Sheet BETHUNE 1/40000
	15.	9pm.	Visited Corps Officers Rest Station & Corps Skin depot and found work proceeding satisfactorily. Much improvement in the cleanliness & arrangements of both. Visited ECOLE CATORIVE & horselines. TENT Subdivision W. R. M. reformed from ECOLE CATORIVE.	
	16	9pm.	Visited D.R.S alongwith G.O.C. 42nd Division + A.D.M.S. 42nd Division. Satisfaction with results obtained in the time. W. R.M.	
	17.	9pm.	Visited Officers Rest Station and SKIN Depot at MERVILLE. W. R. M.	
	18.	9pm.	Visited D.R.S. orders received to close Corps Officers Rest Station and hand over SKIN depot to Field Ambulance of 38th Division.	
	19	9pm.	Corps Officers Rest Station closed. Officers sent to 6 Corps Rest W. R. M. Station & remainder returned to duty. Corps Skin depot to be handed over tomorrow. Visited DRS. at LAPUGNOY. W. R.M.	

A7092 Wt. W128:9/M1293 750,000. 1/17. D. D & I. Ltd. Forms/C2118/14.

Army Form C. 2118.

WAR DIARY
or
~~INTELLIGENCE~~ SUMMARY.
(Erase heading not required.)

Instructions regarding War Diaries and Intelligence Summaries are contained in F. S. Regs., Part II. and the Staff Manual respectively. Title pages will be prepared in manuscript.

Place	Date 1917 DEC.	Hour	Summary of Events and Information	Remarks and references to Appendices
COLLEGE des JEUNNES FILLES BETHUNE	20	10pm.	Handed over Skin Depot to Field Ambulance of 38 Division. Officers and personnel Slipping Depot + Corps Rest Station rejoined unit by route march from MERVILLE today. W.R.M.	REF MAP FRANCE Combined Sheet BETHUNE 1/40,000.
	21.	9pm.	Visited D.R.S. Everything running well & smoothly. 1 NCO + 32 O.R. rejoined unit from 54 C.C.S. W.R.M.	
	22.	9pm.	Nothing special to note. Special arrangements for Xmas being made for patients at D.R.S. + personnel of Field Ambulance at LAPUGNOY and at BETHUNE.	
	23.	9pm.	A.D.M.S. going on leave. OC 1/2 East Lancs Field Ambulance to be acting A.D.M.S. during his absence and Field Ambulance to be under command of CAPTAIN W. J. PURVES.	
	24.	9pm.	Xmas preparations for men + sick D.R.S. Concert ~~at~~ D.R.S. for patients W.R.M.	
	25.	9pm.	Xmas day personnel had dinner at 6pm. Concert after. Officers and N.C.Os. waited on the men. W.R.M.	

A7092 Wt. W125.9/M1293 750,000. 1/17. D. D & L. Ltd. Forms/C2118/14.

Instructions regarding War Diaries and Intelligence Summaries are contained in F. S. Regs., Part II, and the Staff Manual respectively. Title pages will be prepared in manuscript.

WAR DIARY
or
~~INTELLIGENCE SUMMARY.~~
(Erase heading not required.)

Army Form C. 2118.

Place	Date 1917 Dec.	Hour	Summary of Events and Information	Remarks and references to Appendices
COLLEGE des JEUNNES FILLES	26	9pm.	Gas Instruction & Drill. Route march and Camp fatigues. W.R.M.	REF MAP FRANCE Combined Sheet BETHUNE 1/40,000.
	27	9pm.	Gas instruction drill. afternoon gas parade. Orders received for unit to move from BETHUNE to LOCON. (X13. 6.9.5) Transport X7 C.9.8. W.R.M.	
LOCON X13.6.9.5	28	9pm.	Unit moved to LOCON. move completed by 2pm. TRANSPORT to follow as horses not all supplied with frost cogs & roads bad. XV Corps Rest STATION Stores sent to 54 C.C.S. by orders of D.D.M.S. W.R.M.	
	29	9pm.	Nil to report. W.R.M.	
	30	9pm	Route march Baths parade. W.R.M.	
	31	9pm.	Route march. Unit is at present billetted in farms less one section at D.R.S. LAPUGNOY. Health of unit very good. No casualties during the month.	

W.R. Matthews Lt.Col.
Comdg 1/2 East Lanc Fd. Ambce. RAMC TF

A7092 Wt. W128 9/M1293 750,000. 1/17. D. D & L. Ltd. Forms/C2118/14.

1/2nd. East Lancashire Field Ambulance Order No 14.

By Lt. Col W.H.Matthews.R.A.M.C.T.F.

-o-o-o-o-o-o-o-o-o-o-o-o-o-o-o-o-o-o-o-o-o-o-o-o-o-o-o-o-o-o-o-o-o-o-o-o-

Reference Maps 1/40.000 BETHUNE Combined Sheet.
1/10.000 Sheet 36.c.N.W.1.

12.12.17.

1. " B " Section 1/2nd. East Lancashire Field Ambulance will proceed to LA PUGNOY on the 13th. inst and form a Divisional Rest Station at the Camp of No.18 Casualty Clearing Station , and be ready to re ceive patients on 14th. inst. Time of departure to be arranged by O.C. " B " Section.Arrival to be reported to Headquarters of Field Ambulance by Wire.

DRESS.Marching Order, Steel Helmets,P.H.Helmets and Box Respirators to be carried.

TRANSPORT.With the exception of One Water Cart the Transport of "B" section will remain behind.

EQUIPMENT.Only the Medical Equipment of the section will be taken.

Lt. Col.R.A.M.C.T.F.

Commanding 1/2nd. E.L.Field Ambulance.

1 Copy O.C. " B " Section.
1 Copy War Dairy.
1 Copy File.

Confidential

WO 95/2912

140/2095

WAR DIARY OF

1/2ND EAST LANCASHIRE FIELD AMBULANCE.

FROM :- January 1st, 1918: TO :- January 31st, 1918

(VOLUME I)

14

Jan. 1918

Army Form C. 2118.

Instructions regarding War Diaries and Intelligence Summaries are contained in F. S. Regs., Part II. and the Staff Manual respectively. Title pages will be prepared in manuscript.

WAR DIARY
or
~~INTELLIGENCE~~ SUMMARY.

(*Erase heading not required.*)

Place	Date 1918 Jany	Hour	Summary of Events and Information	Remarks and references to Appendices
LOCON X136.9.5	1	9pm	Nothing special to note. Visited A.D.S. + R.A.P. W.R.M.	REF MAP FR. FNCE 1/40,000 BETHUNE Combined Sheet.
	2.	9pm.	Work being carried out at RATION CORNER and PONT FIXE and at ORCHARD RD posts. Satisfactory progress being made. W.R.M.	
	3	9pm	NIL to report. W.R.M.	
LOCON X136.9.5	4.	9pm.	Visited A.D.S. at TUNING FORK and at LONE FARM. Work proceeding satisfactory. New incinerator and drying room + bath house erected at MESPLAUX FARM. W.R.M.	
	5.	9pm.	NIL to report. W.R.M.	
	6	10pm	NIL to report.	
LOCON X136.9.5	7	9pm	Visited A.D.S. and RAP. arranged for anti-gas appliances at A.D.S and RAP. W.R.M.	
	8	10pm	NIL to report W.R.M.	

A7092 Wt. W128.9/M1293 750,000. 1/17. D. D & L. Ltd. Forms/C2118/14.

Instructions regarding War Diaries and Intelligence Summaries are contained in F. S. Regs., Part II. and the Staff Manual respectively. Title pages will be prepared in manuscript.

WAR DIARY

~~or~~

~~INTELLIGENCE SUMMARY.~~

(*Erase heading not required.*)

Army Form C. 2118.

Place	Date 1917 JAN.	Hour	Summary of Events and Information	Remarks and references to Appendices
LOCON X136.95	9	10pm	Visited A.D.S. at TUNING FORK + LONE FARM and RAP at BARNTON ROAD and HARTS REDOUDT + WINDY CORNER also visited the TRENCH FOOT Centre LE PLANTIN. Work at RATON CORNER proceeding satisfactorily but CEMENT short. W. R. M.	REF MAP FRANCE 1/40,000 BETHUNE Combined Sheet.
	10	10pm	Nothing special to report. W. R. M.	
LOCON. X136.9.5	11	10pm	Lt Col. W. R. MATTHEWS O.C. 1/2 East Lanc Field Ambulance appointed to be A.D.M.S. of 42nd Division. Charge of 1/2 East Lanc Fd Ambulance handed over to CAPTAIN J W PURVES 1/2 East Lanc Field Ambce RAMC T.F. The unit was handed over to the O/C in a very fit and efficient state both as regards discipline and appearance as well as in working powers of the personnel of the RAMC and also of the Horse Transport + M.T. W. R. Matthews Lt Col O.C. 1/2 East Lanc Fd Ambce.	

A7092 Wt. W128 9/M1293 750,000. 1/17. D. D & L. Ltd. Forms/C2118/14.

Instructions regarding War Diaries and Intelligence Summaries are contained in F. S. Regs., Part II. and the Staff Manual respectively. Title pages will be prepared in manuscript.

WAR DIARY
or
INTELLIGENCE SUMMARY.
(Erase heading not required.)

Army Form C. 2118.

Place	Date	Hour	Summary of Events and Information	Remarks and references to Appendices
MESPLAUX FARM	11-1-18	6pm	Lieut-Colonel W.R. MATTHEWS D.S.O. RAMC T.F left the unit, and appointed ADMS 42 Div.	W/P
			Capt N.V. PURVES RAMC T.F assumed temporary command.	
			Headquarters Fd Amb. MESPLAUX FARM (BETHUNE combined sheet 36 A) →	X14 A 9.6.
			Personnel Officers 2. OR 118. accomodation for patients 60 cases LYING.	
			A.D.S. LONE FARM (BETHUNE combined sheet 36 A) →	A 7 D.1.2
			personnel Officer 1. OR. 29. accomodation for 20 LYING cases & 50 walking	
			LONE FARM receives from Battalions in the line, also from the support, two RAMC personnel are attached to the Battalion in the line, R.A.P. at Herts Redoubt (M.R) →	[illegible] A 8 D 7.4
			& carry cases to A.D.S. by wheeled stretcher. RELAY POST (M.R) → it acts as a relay	A 14 A 9.8
			to a RAP post on the near side of the canal at PONT A FIX CORNER, also WINDY CORNER which is for the Battalion in support, personnel 4 RAMC, & carry by wheeled stretcher to the ADS LONE FARM. Light railway also laid can be used.	
			BETHUNE combined sheet 36A. F.6.A.5.1. →	F6 A 5.1
			A.D.S. TUNING FORK M.R. BETHUNE combined sheet 36A. accomodation 12 LYING 25 walking	
			personnel Officer 1, OR. 32. cases brought down on a light railway to the A.D.S.	
			R.A.P. 4 RAMC personnel, new A.D.S. at RATION CORNER is in the course of construction, working party of 12 men are now busy.	W/P
MESPLAUX FARM	12-1-18	6pm	Visited ADS LONE FARM Capt. A. GIBSON RAMC T.F in charge, making improvements, laying duck board path, & incinerator at work in the corner of the building	W/P
"	13-1-18	6pm	Visited ADS TUNING FORK Capt N TURNER RAMC T.F in charge	W/P
"	14-1-18	6pm	opened out a Cocoa Stall & Canteen at RATION CORNER instructions from A.D.M.S.	W/P
"	15-1-18	6pm	Building an Incinerator with Drying Room & Bath House combined.	W/P
"	16-1-18	6pm	Capt GIBSON RAMC T.F proceeded on leave, TRANSPORT inspected by the O/C 42 DIV TRAIN	W/P
"	17-1-18	6pm	Lieut Gibbs MORCUSA in charge at LOAN FARM.	W/P

A5834 Wt. W4973/M687 750,000 8/16 D. D. & L. Ltd. Forms/C.2118/13.

Instructions regarding War Diaries and Intelligence Summaries are contained in F. S. Regs., Part II. and the Staff Manual respectively. Title pages will be prepared in manuscript.

WAR DIARY
or
INTELLIGENCE SUMMARY.
(Erase heading not required.)

Army Form C. 2118.

Place	Date	Hour	Summary of Events and Information	Remarks and references to Appendices
MESPLAUX FARM	18-1-18	6pm	Visited ADS LOAN FARM. Lieut Gibbs MRC USA temporary [illegible], Capt H NEAME RAMC T took charge.	[illegible]
"	19-1-18	6pm	Visited ADS TUNING FORK work proceeding at RATION CORNER.	[illegible]
"	20-1-18	6pm	Principal medical work at ADS is the treatment of SCABIES, which are given hot sulphur baths, (POTASS SULPHURATA used)	[illegible]
"	21-1-18	6pm	Routine work.	[illegible]
"	22-1-18	6pm	Routine work	[illegible]
"	23-1-18	6pm	Visited ADS TUNING FORK, work proceeding satisfactorily at RATION CORNER first time an incinerator has been worked at	[illegible]
"	24-1-18	6pm	Visited ADS LOAN FARM, [illegible] smoke [illegible], & has improved the sanitation this ADS, it is working well, of this post being [illegible]	[illegible]
"	25-1-18	6pm	Capt N P MUNROE RAMC T.F arrived from the 16th Fd Amb & took command of the unit.	[illegible]

[illegible]
Capt. RAMC T.F.
1/2 FIELD AMB

A5834 Wt. W4973/M687 750,000 8/16 D. D. & L. Ltd. Forms/C.2118/13.

Instructions regarding War Diaries and Intelligence Summaries are contained in F. S. Regs., Part II. and the Staff Manual respectively. Title pages will be prepared in manuscript.

WAR DIARY
or
INTELLIGENCE SUMMARY.

(Erase heading not required.)

Army Form C. 2118.

Place	Date	Hour	Summary of Events and Information	Remarks and references to Appendices
MESPLAUX FARM	26/1/18	7 pm	Routine duties at M.D.S. The ADMS visited the MDS today. Work proceeding on protection of stables & instruments against aircraft. WTM.	
"	27/1/18	"	Visited ADS at TUNING FORK & RAP at BARNTON ROAD. WTM	
"	28/1/18	"	Visited ADS at LONE FARM & RAPs at WINDY CORNER, HERTS REDOUBT & POINT FIXE. WTM	
"	29/1/18	"	Routine duties. WTM	
"	30/1/18	"	Routine: material being arrived for the erection of walls to protect stables against bombs from aircraft, the work is now in hand. Material indented for, for protection of the instruments. Improvements being carried on at both A.D. Stations, & work being carried on at the new ADS. at RATION CORNER. WTM. The officers at present at HQ are Capt MUNRO, Capt PURVES, Capt NEAME & QMr & Hon Lieut LOWE. WTM	
"	31/1/18	"	Routine. Personnel paid. WTM.	

[illegible]
Capt RAMC
OC. 1/2 East Lancs Fd Ambce.

A5834 Wt. W4973/M687 750,000 8/16 D. D. & L. Ltd. Forms/C.2118/13.

W A R   D I A R Y

OF

1/2nd EAST LANCASHIRE FIELD AMBULANCE.

FROM :- February 1st, 1918 TO :- February 28th, 1918.

(VOLUME 2)

Army Form C. 2118.

Instructions regarding War Diaries and Intelligence Summaries are contained in F. S. Regs., Part II. and the Staff Manual respectively. Title pages will be prepared in manuscript.

WAR DIARY
or
INTELLIGENCE SUMMARY.
(Erase heading not required.)

Place	Date	Hour	Summary of Events and Information	Remarks and references to Appendices
MESPLAUX FARM Nr. LOCON	Feby 1	7/1m	Routine. Preparation of "scheme of training" for the personnel when in the [illegible] WTM	
"	Feby 2	"	Routine. Visited TUNING FORK + RAP Barnton Road today. WTM	
"	Feby 3	"	Routine. One wounded passed through our hands during preceding 24 hours. WTM	
"	Feby 4	"	Routine. One wounded: Visited TUNING FORK + LONE FARM A.D.Stations. Lieut BREWER M.O.R.C.U.S.A. was transferred yesterday to 1/1 F.A. + struck off our strength WTM	
"	Feby 5	"	Routine. Weekly S.B.R. Inspection Drill. WTM	
"	Feby 6	"	Routine 3 wounded. Visited TUNING FORK + area. WTM	
"	Feby 7	"	Routine 2 wounded. Visited LONE FARM + RAPs + Tuning Fork ADS WTM	
"	Feby 8	"	Routine 3 wounded. Sent to [illegible] Battalions [illegible] WTM.	
"	Feby 9	"	Routine: 2 wounded. Orders drawn up for Orderly Officer, Orderly Sergeant, Corporal of the guard & Standing Orders for unit. WTM	
"	Feby 10	"	Sunday. 1 wounded. Visited LONE FARM & TUNING FORK A.D.Stations + RAP at HERTS Redoubt + WINDY CORNER WTM. Capt TURNER proceeded for temp duty with [illegible] + Lt Brewer USA M.R.C. was attached to this unit for temp. duty. WTM.	
"	Feby 11	"	Attended F.A. Commanders Conference at A.D.M.S. Office. Advance party of 1 NCO + 6 men proceeded to 1st Corps Scabies Station. Advance parties arrived from 2/1st West Lancs F.A. and proceeded to the A.D.Stations. No wounded. WTM	
"	Feby 12	"	Routine. Wounded 2 officers 9 O.R. 3 German prisoners result of raid on enemy trenches. Medical arrangements worked satisfactorily. WTM. Capt [illegible] + 20 O.R. proceeded for duty to 1st Corps C.S.S.	
CANTRAINNE	Feby 13	"	Unit moved today to CANTRAINNE, 1½ miles E. of LILLERS. Relieved by 2/1st W. Lancs F.A. Transport travelled well. [illegible] at MESPLAUX FARM to be used by the 126 I.B. WTM	
"	Feby 14	"	Capt GIBSON RAMC T.F. proceeded with details to CSS for duty. WTM	
"	Feby 15	"	General Fatigues. Personnel paid. Brigade sick collected from villages BUSNES, BUSNETTE LECLEME + AINGETTE. WTM.	

A5834 Wt. W4973/M687 750,000 8/16 D. D. & L. Ltd. Forms/C.2118/13.

Instructions regarding War Diaries and Intelligence Summaries are contained in F. S. Regs., Part II. and the Staff Manual respectively. Title pages will be prepared in manuscript.

WAR DIARY
or
INTELLIGENCE SUMMARY.
(Erase heading not required.)

Army Form C. 2118.

Place	Date	Hour	Summary of Events and Information	Remarks and references to Appendices
CANTRAILLES	16/2/18	7pm	Conference at ADMS re training, scabies prevention &c. Inspection of men's boots & clothing. Capt PURVIS returned to HQ from CSS & Lt. DICKINSON from 1/5 Lancs Fusiliers. Lt Brewer proceeded to C.S.S. & report to Capt GIBSON. WHM	
"	17/2/18	"	Church Parades. WHM	
"	18/2/18	"	Training begun. Company drill, Stretcher drill, Lecture on "Haemorrhage" & Instruction in medical & surg. WHM	
"	19/2/18	"	Training continued. ADMS conference at FA with Brig. Staff Captain regimental MOs & FA MOs re Scabies & "Shock". WHM	
"	20/2/18	"	Training continued. Half Holiday. Sports. WHM. Lieut LOWE RAMC returned from Leave today. WHM	
"	21/2/18	"	Baths for men at LILLERS. General Fatigues. WHM	
"	22/2/18	"	Training continued. DMS (Surg. Gen. THOMPSON) inspected Corps Scabies Station today & expressed satisfaction with the working of the place. WHM	
"	23/2/18	"	Training continued. Afternoon Sports football. At present at HQ the officers are besides myself Capt PURVIS, Capt NEAME & Lieut DICKINSON MORCUSA. At the Scabies Station Capt GIBSON & Lieut BREWER MORCUSA attached. Capt TURNER at RAMC School. Capt WEBSTER is still with the Div Concert Party. Capt GIBBS USA is MO i/c Reinforcement camp. About 40 OR are at Scabies Station & about 22 O.R. at the Div. Concert Party. Capt NEAME sees the sick & supervises sanitation of 1/5 E Lancs Regt. Lieut Dickinson that of 126 TMB & 3rd Employment Battn. at BUSNES. WHM	
"	24/2/18	"	Church Parades. Sports. WHM.	
"	25/2/18	"	Training continued. Weather not very favourable. Lectures given chiefly today. WHM	
"	26/2/18	"	Training continued. SBRs inspected & Gas Drill. WHM	
"	27/2/18	"	Training continued. Half Holiday.	
"	28/2/18	"	Training continued. Address by Col. CLIVE Gren. Gds re War Loan.	

W H [illegible] Lt Col.
RAMC TF
OC 1/2nd East Lancs Fd Ambce.

A5834 Wt. W4973/M687 750,000 8/16 D. D. & L. Ltd. Forms/C.2118/13.

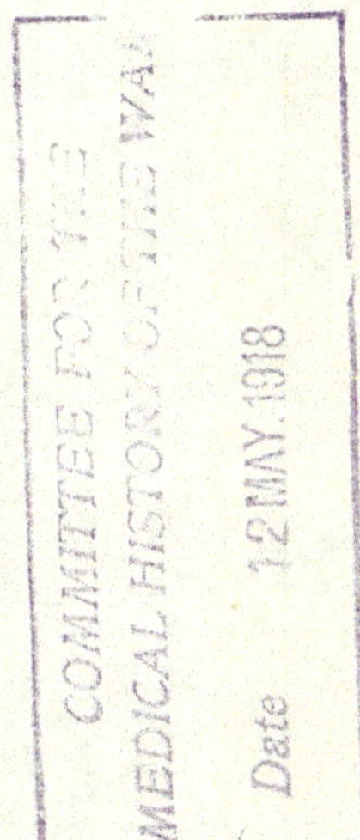

WAR DIARY

OF

1/2nd East Lancashire FIELD AMBULANCE, R.A.M.C.(T.F.)

FROM :- March 1st, 1918 TO :- March 31st, 1918.

(VOLUME 111)

Army Form C. 2118.

Instructions regarding War Diaries and Intelligence Summaries are contained in F. S. Regs., Part II. and the Staff Manual respectively. Title pages will be prepared in manuscript.

WAR DIARY
or
INTELLIGENCE SUMMARY.
(Erase heading not required.)

Place	Date	Hour	Summary of Events and Information	Remarks and references to Appendices
CANTRAINNE	March 1	7pm	Training continued. Arrangements being made to take over 1st Corps Scabies Stn to an ambulance of 40th Div. Capt WEBSTER now relieved for duty to units. DFM.	
"	2	"	Stretcher Bearers returned from various battalions today. Training continued & packing the wagons. DFM.	
"	3	"	wagons inspected. DFM. Capt TURNER returned from 1st ARMY RAMC School. DFM	
"	4	"	Conference of FA Commanders at ADMS office. 126th IB moved from BUSNES area to BURBURE area. The FA is now responsible for collection of 127th IB sick who are in the BUSNES area — the Div. Artillery which is in the Ham-en-Artois area. DFM	
"	5	"	Training continued.	
"	6	"	Training continued. The 1st Corps Scabies Station was taken over today by the 1/1st North Mid. Fd Amb. & Capt GIBSON & party have returned to HQ. We have still got a few scabies patients undergoing treatment in the FA. the scabies station being still closed. At present the officers at the HQ consist of the O.C. Capt PURVES Capt WEBSTER, Capt TURNER Capt GIBSON Capt NEAME & Qr Mr & Hon Lieut. LOWE Lieut DICKINSON MORCUSA. is still m.o. i/c 42nd Div Wing at ALLOUAGNE. Capt TURNER is from tomorrow detailed as m.o. i/c 8th MANCHESTER Regt. Capt WEBSTER sees the sick of the 127th TMB. daily. Cars in workshop — two Fords. A Daimler goes for inspection each third day. Men in comfortable billets which are barns. Weather fine. DFM.	
"	7	"	Training continued. D. F. Munroe Lt Col.	
"	8	7pm	Lieut-Col. W.F. MUNROE M.C. on leave, Capt. N. J. PURVES took temporary Command. Training continued, one case of Diphtheria from 1/6 MANCH. Location L'ECLEME. W.J.P.	
"	9	7p.m.	Training continued, two G.S. loads of shale from BRUAY for improving Horse Standings. 101 CHINESE LABOUR CORP camped in the QUARRY near HAUTRIEUX seen by Capt. CA WEBSTER re sick. W.J.P.	

A5834 Wt. W4973/M687 750,000 8/16 D. D. & L. Ltd. Forms/C.2118/13.

Instructions regarding War Diaries and Intelligence Summaries are contained in F. S. Regs., Part II. and the Staff Manual respectively. Title pages will be prepared in manuscript.

WAR DIARY
or
INTELLIGENCE SUMMARY.
(Erase heading not required.)

Army Form C. 2118.

Place	Date	Hour	Summary of Events and Information	Remarks and references to Appendices
CENTRAINNE	March 10	7p.m.	Conference at ADMS office, decided that each Fd Amb commander superintends the Brigade area, also that the Brassard be worn for ceremonial purposes. Red cross be painted on the G.S. wagons, Limber wagons, and water carts.	W.P.
"	11	7pm	Training continued, ADMS, C/o 1/1 Fd Amb & myself visited the northern sector occupied by the 1st Division of the Portuguese troops. Main Dressing stations LA GORGUE L. 34 B 9.2, and L 36 A 0.9 Map Ref 36 A. A.D.S. LAVENTIE then in front of the ADS you pass a walking wounded post on the left known as STEEL SHELTER about 1 mile from the ADS. forward again you come to a Collecting post known as RED FARM, a big stone building with very small accomodation for sick or wounded, mainly occupied by Battalion Headquarters, not a good arrangement. forward again you find the R.A.Ps known as HYDEPARK M.7.A.8.8 and WHITE HOUSE M12 C 25, 33. this arrangement is with the Left Bgd. A.D.S. L'EPINETTE Map Ref. M16 D 7.7. forward from there you come to R.A.P known as WINCHESTER POST M 23 A 43, 05. Roads are good, cars can get along, light trench railway running from Red Farm to the trenches.	36 a.m. Steel Shelter M5A705 M6D21 W.P.
"	12	7pm	Training Routine.	W.P.
"	13	7pm	Training Routine, RAMC contest for the best turned out LIMBER from the Fd Amb's of 42 DIV, 1/2 Fd Amb won.	W.P.

Army Form C. 2118.

Instructions regarding War Diaries and Intelligence Summaries are contained in F. S. Regs., Part II. and the Staff Manual respectively. Title pages will be prepared in manuscript.

WAR DIARY
or
INTELLIGENCE SUMMARY.
(Erase heading not required.)

Place	Date	Hour	Summary of Events and Information	Remarks and references to Appendices
CHATRAINNE	14	7pm	A.D.M.S. O/C 1/1 Fd Amb & myself visited the Southern Sector occupied by the 2nd Div of the PORTUGESE TROOPS. M.D.Ss ZELOBES R 27 C 2.4. LATOMBE-WILLOT R 31.C 8.2. Map Ref. 36a combined A D Ss RUE DE BOIS X 17 central, GREEN BARN M 27. D 5.2, ST VAAST M 32 D 8.3 Map Ref 36a Comb. R.A.Ps PATH POST S14 B 8.3 WINDER CORNER SQ A 859, LANSDOWNE POST S3 D 9.7 CURZON POINT M 34 B 35 Map Refs 36A Combined Light trench railways running between the A.D.Ss & R.A.Ps Conference at A.D.M.S Office at 4.30 p.m. decided to discard the [illegible] for the A.S.C. men attached, A.S.C men be given a course of musketry. Question of movement by Tactical or Strategical Train, Equipment [illegible] to carry.	W/D
"	15	7pm	Training Routine. Two G.S. limbered waggons packed for movement to Tactical Train. Field Ambulance now up to strength, Concert party & fatigue men returned from ALLOUAGNE	W/D
"	16	7pm	Training Routine, A. KEELING 1st class N.O. detailed for duty with the 83 Squadron R.F.C.	W/D
	17	7pm	Conference A.D.M.S Office decided to send A.S.C. men to the Div WING for training, also to make arrangements with Brigade to allow them a course of musketry.	W/D
"	18	7pm	Training Routine. MOTOR AMBULANCE & HORSE AMBULANCE equipment checked.	W/D

A5834 Wt. W4973/M687 750,000 8/16 D. D. & L. Ltd. Forms/C.2118/13.

Instructions regarding War Diaries and Intelligence Summaries are contained in F. S. Regs., Part II. and the Staff Manual respectively. Title pages will be prepared in manuscript.

WAR DIARY
or
INTELLIGENCE SUMMARY.
(Erase heading not required.)

Army Form C. 2118.

Place	Date	Hour	Summary of Events and Information	Remarks and references to Appendices
CANTRAINNE	19	7pm	Training Routine, visited the H.Q. of 1/7 MANCH. BUSNES, 1/6 MANCH. L'ECLEME 1/5 MANCH BUNETTE. Lt. DICKINSON. MORC.U.S.A left for leave to ENGLAND, Capt. NEAME W/P took Medical charge of the 42 Div.-Wing.	Map 36 A Combined
"	20	7pm.	Training Routine, W/P	
"	21	7pm.	Training Routine, W/P	
"	22	7pm	Training Routine, W/P	
"	23	7pm	127 BRIGADE moved from CANTRAINNE to AYETTE by Bus, left CANTRAINNE 10.30 A.M. arrived AYETTE 2 A.M. 24-3-18. Embussing point was on the LILLERS – BUSNES Road, 20 men in the LORRIES 25 in BUSSES. Officers with main body Major PURVES & Capt. GIBSON, Lieut. LOWE went on in advance on a MOTOR AMBULANCE with 4 O.R. RATIONS were carried for the 23rd on the man, 24th in bulk, divided the weight amongst the men. TRANSPORT moved by road under MAJOR WEBSTER, one Motor Lorry was detailed to bring surplus baggage. Motor Ambs moved in a convoy from the three Field Ambs under D.A.D.M.S. Camped in huts at the AYETTE AERODROME, near 127 BRIGADE Advance party arrived about 8.30pm, prepared some tea, which was ready when the main body marched in at 2pm on the 24th/3/18 W/P	Map Ref

A5834 Wt. W4973/M687 750,000 8/16 D. D. & L. Ltd. Forms/C.2118/13.

Instructions regarding War Diaries and Intelligence Summaries are contained in F. S. Regs., Part II. and the Staff Manual respectively. Title pages will be prepared in manuscript.

WAR DIARY
or
INTELLIGENCE SUMMARY.
(Erase heading not required.)

Army Form C. 2118.

Place	Date	Hour	Summary of Events and Information	Remarks and references to Appendices
AYETTE	March 24	7pm.	127 Bgd under orders to take over part of the line in front of GOMIECOURT, detailed 1 corp. and 8 men to march off and report to the M.O. of 1/5, 1/6, 1/7 MANCH[S]. these bearers left our lines at 7-30 p.m. marched off with light kit, 1 corp & 8 men with each battalion. Remaining bearers were handed over to the C.O. of 1/1 Field Amb: who was running the line. Headquarters and three Tent Sub. Div[s] of this unit were under orders to take over from the 135 FD AMB, the MAIN DRESSING STATION at AYETTE, which was once an INDIAN HOSPITAL. W.P.	Maps Ref
AYETTE	25	7pm	MOVED from the AERODROME at 8-30 A.M. & rested outside the INDIAN HOSPITAL, saw the C.O. of the 135 FD AMB, who was waiting for instructions from his A.D.M.S. TOOK over the M.D.S. at 12-30 mid-day. Officers at the M.D.S. MAJOR PURVES, MAJOR WEBSTER, CAPTAIN GIBSON, LIEUT LONG MORUSA. WOUNDED were evacuated in M.A.C cars to the 43 C.C.S. This C.C.S. was gradually clearing out, & many of the cases had to go on to DOULLENS STATIONARY HOSPITAL, the distance being so great & the traffic so congested, the MAC cars were held up, in consequence I did not get the stretcher cases away as soon as one would have liked. W.P.	

A5834 Wt. W4973/M687 750,000 8/16 D. D. & L. Ltd. Forms/C.2118/13.

Instructions regarding War Diaries and Intelligence Summaries are contained in F. S. Regs., Part II. and the Staff Manual respectively. Title pages will be prepared in manuscript.

WAR DIARY
or
INTELLIGENCE SUMMARY.
(Erase heading not required.)

Army Form C. 2118.

Place	Date	Hour	Summary of Events and Information	Remarks and references to Appendices
AYETTE	March 25	7pm	The numbers we were faced to deal with, I found it impossible to give A.T. Serum at the M.D.S. So marked on the card that it had not been given. The walking wounded were sent down in MOTOR LORRIES. Some delay took place owing to the fact that no LORRIES were attached to the M.D.S. ADMS after being informed, had six [illegible] found them most useful. Evacuated Officers 40, 834, O.R.s Capt TURNER who was attached temporarily for duty with the [illegible] was evacuated sick. W.P.	Hosp Ref
AYETTE	26	7pm	The M.D.S. was cleared of all WOUNDED & SICK, and closed as a M.D.S. it was too near the enemy lines, & guns in the open were placed all around. All the stretchers, blankets, medical stores were removed, & under instructions from the ADMS the unit moved back to LA CAUCHIE, & took over the camp vacated by the 4th AUSTRALIAN FD Amb. Evacuated 240 and cleared the M.D.S. Lieut. Col. MONROE M.C. returned from leave and took over command of the Unit. W.P.	

Instructions regarding War Diaries and Intelligence Summaries are contained in F. S. Regs., Part II. and the Staff Manual respectively. Title pages will be prepared in manuscript.

WAR DIARY
or
INTELLIGENCE SUMMARY.
(Erase heading not required.)

Army Form C. 2118.

Place	Date	Hour	Summary of Events and Information	Remarks and references to Appendices
LACAUCHIE	Mch 26	7pm	HQ of 7A moved to LACAUCHIE, about 100 men accomodated in huts, preparing to form MDS if necessary. One Daimler car at HQ. Horse transport at BAC de SUD on Arras Doullens road. Remainder of bearers with OC No 1 7A. WTn	
"	27	"	About 20 cases chiefly walking cases evacuated from this Station. Officers present are Self, Major Purves, Major Wilets + Capt Gibson. The 3 H. ambulances proceeded to OC No 1 7A at Monchy. Major Purves proceeded to Bac de Sud to form a W. W Post with a few men WTn	
"	28	"	Capt Gibson proceeded to No 3 7A for temporary duty. About 30 cases chiefly walking cases (sick + wounded) are sent in charge of RAMC NCO. to Arras Doullens road to await motor lorries returning to Doullens	
"	29	"	MDS opened at LACAUCHIE About 12 MAC cars attached. WTn	
GAUDIEMPRE	30	"	Unit proceeded to GAUDIEMPRE today having been relieved by 140 7A of 41st Div. MDS opened at this village + 6 MAC cars attached belonging to 12 MAC. One of our own Daimlers with us + of H.T. one water cart one limbered wagon + two riders. The rest of HT at HENU under Lieut LOWE. The dump of medical stores removed to Gaudiempre. 3 motor lorries attached for carrying walking wounded cases. Capt Gibson returned with the bearers this afternoon WTn	
"	31	"	About 101 cases wounded passed through MDS today ^since 6pm yesterday to 6pm tonight^ ~~[illegible]~~ Conference at ADMS of 7A Commanders this afternoon. Dump proposed at Doullens to store equipment surplus to establishment + C DPM. Officers at MDS include self, Major Purves, Major Wilets, Major Bucknall + Lieut Hale MORCUSA. Capt Gibson. Lieut Lowe at Transport Lines. WTn	
	AF		[signature] Lt Col. 1/2nd East Lancs Fd Amb	

A7092 Wt W128 9/M1293 750,000. 1/17. D. D & L., Ltd. Forms/C2118/14.

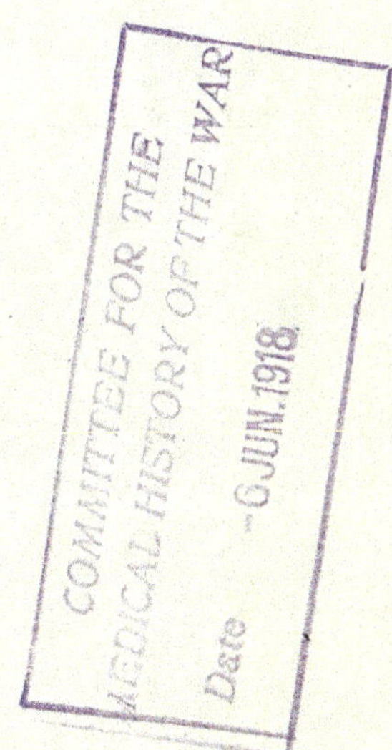

W A R D I A R Y

OF

1/2ND EAST LANCASHIRE FIELD AMBULANCE

FROM :- April 1st, 1918 TO :- April 30th, 1918.

(VOLUME IV)

Army Form C. 2118.

Instructions regarding War Diaries and Intelligence Summaries are contained in F. S. Regs., Part II. and the Staff Manual respectively. Title pages will be prepared in manuscript.

WAR DIARY
or
INTELLIGENCE SUMMARY.

(Erase heading not required.)

Place	Date	Hour	Summary of Events and Information	Remarks and references to Appendices
GUARLEMPRE	April 1	7pm	Men bathed in village. Kits & clothing inspected WTM	
SOUASTRE	2	–	50 bearers under Capt GIBSON proceeded at midnight to report to OC 3rd FA for duty & other 30 under Major WEBSTER at 6 am for same purpose. Unit moved to SOUASTRE today taking over billets of 1st E L F A. The most of our surgical dressings & splints sent to OC No 1 FA who is now running the MDS at LA CAUCHIE. The 3rd FA does the forward area & we run a dressing station for local ~~sick &~~ wounded. Major BRENTNALL returned to No 1 FA last night. Dump formed at DOULLENS for keeping extra equipment & stores of the FA. WTM	
"	3	"	Sick Parades of local units seen. Lieut. SERGEANT ~~[illegible]~~ RAMC (T.C) reported last evening for duty. WTM DDMS 4th Corps visited units' buildings today WTM	
"	4	"	Routine. Capt NEAME returned from 1/1st E L F A today WTM	
"	5	"	Routine. About 70 cases (lying & sitting wounded) were accommodated in our dressing station today & evacuated. Unit moved to billet in village, the old site being handed over to 1/1st [?] FA who are forming a MDS there. Another 25 men sent up as bearers to 1/3rd FA at BIENVILLERS. WTM.	
"	6	"	Major WEBSTER having returned to HQ, Capt NEAME & Lieut DICKENSON MORC proceeded to 1/3 FA. Capt GIBSON returned this afternoon. WTM	
"	7	"	Unit moved today to MARIEUX Aerodrome. Arrangements being made for collection of sick of 125th IB. WTM	
"	8	"	Most of bearers returned to unit during night. Orders to move ~~[illegible]~~ today to LOUVENCOURT which was cancelled later. Weather very wet at present WTM	

Instructions regarding War Diaries and Intelligence Summaries are contained in F. S. Regs., Part II. and the Staff Manual respectively. Title pages will be prepared in manuscript.

WAR DIARY
or
INTELLIGENCE SUMMARY.

(Erase heading not required.)

Army Form C. 2118.

Place	Date	Hour	Summary of Events and Information	Remarks and references to Appendices
MARIEUX	9/4/18	7pm	Conference of FA commanders at ADMS office PAS. Unit moved to MARIEUX. New billets in barns. Sick of 127 IB. at LOUVENCOURT collected. WTM	
"	10/4/18	"	Arrangements made for bathing personnel at SARTON. [illegible] WTM	
"	11/4/18	"	Certain amount of medical [illegible] dumped at DOULLENS. Scabies cases of IB treated in hospital which is in barn.	
"	12/4/18	"	Inspection of 127 IB & FA at VAUCHELLES at midday. Conference of F.A. commanders at ADMS office 4 pm. WTM	
"	13/4/18	"	Major PURVES & self reconnoitred SARTON & ORVILLE & AMPLIER with a view to selecting MDS. Most suitable place found in AMPLIER at W end of village. Chateau on one side of road & Paper mill on other, both with cellars. Capt WEBSTER A.D. posted to 1/2 E L FA. WTM	
"	14/4/18	"	Routine. Church Parade. WTM.	
"	15/4/18	"	Relief taking place today of Fd Ambulance of 37th Div running ADS at FONQUEVILLERS & bearer posts. WTM	
"	16/4/18	"	FONQUEVILLERS ADS & bearer posts relieved this morning 6 a.m. Relief of SAILLY-au-Bois ADS taking place. WTM	
BAYENCOURT	17/4/18	"	HQ of FA moved to BAYENCOURT. 3 H[illegible] ambulance stationed here with [illegible]. Transport lines at "Happy Valley" COUIN. WTM	
"	18/4/18	"	Arrangements made for 40 bearers of 1/1st FA to be attached to us at BAYENCOURT to act as reserve for bearers at SAILLY. WTM	
"	19/4/18	"	Conference at ADMS office of F.A. commanders. WTM	
"	20/4/18	"	Routine. WTM	
"	21/4/18	"	Routine. WTM	

Army Form C. 2118.

WAR DIARY
or
INTELLIGENCE SUMMARY.
(Erase heading not required.)

Instructions regarding War Diaries and Intelligence Summaries are contained in F. S. Regs., Part II. and the Staff Manual respectively. Title pages will be prepared in manuscript.

Place	Date	Hour	Summary of Events and Information	Remarks and references to Appendices
BAYENCOURT	Ap 22/18	7 pm	Routine. ADMS of NZ Div visited ADS SAILLY with a view to one of his ambulances taking over this station on the [illegible] posts etc. WTM	
"	23	"	Routine. One A.S.C. attached wounded at Transport Lines COUIN. WTM	
"	24	"	ADS SAILLY-au-BOIS relieved by [illegible] FA ~~[illegible]~~ N.Z. AMC. WTM.	
"	25	"	Visited ADS FONQUEVILLERS + the 6 RAPs of the 125 + 126 Bdes. WTM	
"	26	"	Sent about 65 [illegible] to Transport lines. Routine WTM	
"	27	"	Routine. ADS work progressing at FONQUEVILLERS. WTM Major [illegible] proceeded on 14 days special leave. WTM	
SOUASTRE	28	"	H.Q. of unit moved to SOUASTRE this morning opening at 11 a.m. [illegible] Sergeant left at BAYENCOURT with one Car + about 17 OR. Capt WEBSTER at HQ. Capt GIBSON + Lieut GIBBS at Transport lines with QM LOWE. Major WEBSTER Capt NEAME + Capt ROBERTS att 1/1 FA are at ADS FONQUEVILLERS.	
			Major [illegible] awarded M.C. 5 Military Medals awarded other ranks serving in the ambulance. WTM	
"	29	"	Routine. WTM.	
"	30	"	Routine. ADMS of 57th Div visited ADS this morning. WTM	

[illegible signature]
Lt Col.
OC 1/2 East Lancs Fd Ambulance

WAR DIARY

OF

1/2nd EAST LANCASHIRE FIELD AMBULANCE.

FROM :- May 1st, 1918. TO :- May 31st, 1918.

(VOLUME V)

Instructions regarding War Diaries and Intelligence Summaries are contained in F. S. Regs., Part II. and the Staff Manual respectively. Title pages will be prepared in manuscript.

WAR DIARY
or
INTELLIGENCE SUMMARY.
(Erase heading not required.)

Army Form C. 2118.

Place	Date	Hour	Summary of Events and Information	Remarks and references to Appendices
SOUASTRE	May 1	7pm	Routine. DMS 3rd Army visited HQ to-day. WTM	
"	2	"	Routine. Showed the ADMS & OC relieving Fd Ambce round forward area. WTM	
"	3	"	Arranged with OC relieving FA details of relief. Conference of FA Commanders at ADMS Office. WTM	
"	4	"	Routine. Moved staff of bearers at ADS & posts by 37 today. Two bearers attached to RFA (210 Bde D Batty) killed by shell yesterday. WTM	
"	5	"	Routine. WTM. Relief of ADS & Bearer Posts begun by 2/3rd WESSEX Fd Ambce 57th Div. WTM	
HENU	6	"	Relief in progress. H-Q relieved. Bayencourt relieved. & Happy Valley Transport lines relieved. HQ now at HENU with transport lines. WTM	
"	7	"	Collection of 9 B sick (127 9 B)	
"	8	"	Conference at ADMS office. WTM	
"	9	"	at 7.55 today received order "Practise Battle Positions" Major WEBSTER with two officers one bearer subdivision & portion of a tent subdivision the Fd. Ambulance one limber GS wagon one m. cyclist & 4 stretcher carriers proceeded to SOUASTRE found a hypothetical ADS & reconnoitred routes if the Red Line was being held with outposts on SAILLY – Chateau Haie Switch. Report & suggestions forwarded to ADMS. Weather now fine. WTM	
	10	"	Conference at ADMS office re yesterdays battle practice. WTM	
	11	"	Routine. [illegible] Slightly sick detained [illegible] billets [illegible] WTM	
"	12	"	Church Parades. WTM	
"	13	"	Routine WTM	
"	14	"	Routine. WTM	
"	15	"	Routine WTM	

Army Form C. 2118.

Instructions regarding War Diaries and Intelligence Summaries are contained in F. S. Regs., Part II. and the Staff Manual respectively. Title pages will be prepared in manuscript.

WAR DIARY
or
INTELLIGENCE SUMMARY.
(Erase heading not required.)

Place	Date	Hour	Summary of Events and Information	Remarks and references to Appendices
HENU	Aug 16/18	7pm	Routine. The village was bombed last evening about 10.30 pm; 27 casualties passed through our F.A. chiefly from 3rd ~~[illegible]~~ Bn. Manchester Regt. WTM	
"	Aug 17/18	--	Routine. Employed motor lorry to evacuate sitting cases many of whom were N.Z. troops. One [illegible]. WTM	
"	Aug 18/18	--	Routine. WTM	
"	Aug 19/18	--	Routine + Church Parade. WTM	
"	Aug 20/18	--	Routine. WTM.	
"	Aug 21/18	--	Routine. WTM.	
"	Aug 22/18	--	Routine. Most of personnel equipped today with triplex [illegible] for [illegible]. WTM	
"	Aug 23/18	--	Routine. WTM	
"	Aug 24/18	--	Routine. WTM. Lieut SARGEANT proceeded for temporary duty as M.O. i/c [illegible] Regt. WTM	
"	Aug 25/18	--	Routine. WTM	
"	Aug 26/18	--	Routine. Presentation of Medal Ribbons to recipients of recent awards. WTM	
"	Aug 27/18	--	Routine. Inspection of H.T. by O.C. Train. WTM	
"	Aug 28/18	"	Routine. Inventories of personnel being dealt with. WTM	
"	Aug 29/18	--	Routine. Sports (Ambulance) during afternoon. WTM	
"	Aug 30/18	--	Routine.	
"	Aug 31/18	--	Routine. During the month improvements have been made in camp including new [illegible] baths, scabies treatment &c. At present following officers are with unit: O.C., [illegible], Major [illegible], Capts [illegible] Gibson, Lieut Gibbs & Lieut Towle QM. Lieut Sargeant is with [illegible] & Capt [illegible] at 3 Canadian Stat. Hospital.	

[illegible] Lt Col.

A7092 Wt. W128 9/M1293 750,000. 1/17. D. D & L. Ltd. Forms/C2118/14.

W A R   D I A R Y

OF

1/2nd EAST LANCASHIRE FIELD AMBULANCE.

FROM :- JUNE 1st, 1918 TO :- JUNE 30th, 1918.

(VOLUME VI)

Instructions regarding War Diaries and Intelligence Summaries are contained in F. S. Regs., Part II. and the Staff Manual respectively. Title pages will be prepared in manuscript.

WAR DIARY
or
INTELLIGENCE SUMMARY.

(*Erase heading not required.*)

Army Form C. 2118.

Place	Date	Hour	Summary of Events and Information	Remarks and references to Appendices
HENU	June 1/18	7pm	Routine. Half day holiday for personnel as far as possible. WTM	
"	June 2/18	4pm	Routine & Church Parades. WTM	
"	June 3/18	–	Routine. With Major Webster & Lieut Lane visited MDS (NZ) at BUS preparatory to taking over from them. WTM	
"	June 4/18	–	Routine. WTM	
"	June 5/18	–	Routine. Major Webster proceeded this afternoon to BUS en ARTOIS with about 10 O.R. as an advance party preparatory to our taking over MDS there which is now [illegible] by the 1st NZ F.Amb. WTM	
"	June 6/18	–	Routine. Packing wagons preparatory to move tomorrow. Capt Gibson proceeded this day for temporary duty with 6th Batt. Manchester Regt. WTM	
BUS in ARTOIS	June 7/18	–	Relieved 1st NZ Fd Ambce 12 midday ~~[illegible]~~ today at the M.D.S. The 1/1st run the forward area, the 1/3rd run the DRS & also arrange for lightly wounded cases to proceed by rail from LOUVENCOURT. There are 5 RAMC ~~[illegible]~~ of our unit with each batt: of the 127th Bde. Lieut Sergeant is still with the 5th East Lancs, Lieut Gibbs has proceeded as M.O. i/c 293 Bde RFA (A.T). Our transport is partly at BUS & partly at LOUVENCOURT. WTM	
"	June 8/18	–	Routine. Improvement of camp. 21 wounded. WTM	
"	June 9/18	–	Routine. Mild epidemic of PUO (probably influenza) has broken out among the personnel, about 12 in[cluding] 2 officers affected. All necessary steps taken to prevent its spread & ADMS has been notified. WTM	
"	June 10/18	–	Routine. 6 wounded passed through MDS during previous 24 hours. WTM	
"	June 11/18	–	Routine. 6 wounded – – – Gas centre being arranged for in the village. WTM	
"	June 12/18	–	Routine. 1 wounded (who died in MDS). About 30 personnel have been affected with "influenza" but most recover after 72 hours. WTM	

A7092 Wt W128 9/M1293 750,000 1/17. D. D & L., Ltd. Forms/C2118/14.

Army Form C. 2118.

Instructions regarding War Diaries and Intelligence Summaries are contained in F. S. Regs., Part II. and the Staff Manual respectively. Title pages will be prepared in manuscript.

WAR DIARY
or
INTELLIGENCE SUMMARY.
(Erase heading not required.)

Place	Date	Hour	Summary of Events and Information	Remarks and references to Appendices
BUS in ARTOIS	June 13-18	7 pm	Routine. 1 officer + 6 O.R. wounded. [illegible] passed through MDS WTM	
"	June 14.18	"	" 3 wounded passed through MDS. DDMS IV Corps visited MDS today & expressed approval WTM	
"	June 15	"	Routine. (1 officer 18 OR wounded/[illegible]) WTM	
"	June 16	"	Routine. Church Parade (2 officers + 25 OR + 1 German soldier wounded), a [illegible] having been done this morning by [illegible] of the battalions in the line WTM	
"	June 17	"	Routine. Lieut Sergeant proceeds to 3rd [illegible] for Temp Duty. WTM (2 O. + 10 O.R. wounded) WTM	
"	June 18	"	Routine (5 O R Wounded) Capt. O'DRISCOLL RAMC (SR) reports for duty today. Improvements being continued in the camp. WTM	
"	June 19	"	Routine. (2 Off + 42 OR wounded chiefly 5th [illegible] who were being [illegible] this morning) WTM	
"	June 20	"	Routine (11 OR wounded) WTM	
"	June 21	"	Routine (5 O.R. wounded) Gas Centre nearing completion as also new latrines, & new store room for patients awaiting evacuation. WTM	
"	June 22	"	Routine (1 officer + 5 OR wounded) weather during last 3 days wet & windy. [illegible] yesterday 30 men proceed to site of reserve ADS to dig [illegible] WTM	
"	June 23	"	Routine. Church services (4 O.R. wounded) WTM	
"	June 24	"	Routine (2 OR wounded) arrangements being made to form dugout (gas proof) for stretcher cases WTM	
"	June 25	"	Routine. (9 OR wounded) Dugouts begun at MDS. WTM	
	June 26	"	Routine. (5 OR wounded) [illegible] WTM	
	June 27		Routine (1 officer + 10 OR) WTM	

A7092. Wt W128 9/M1293 750,000. 1/17. D. D & L., Ltd. Forms/C2118/14.

Instructions regarding War Diaries and Intelligence Summaries are contained in F. S. Regs., Part II. and the Staff Manual respectively. Title pages will be prepared in manuscript.

WAR DIARY
or
INTELLIGENCE SUMMARY.

(Erase heading not required.)

Army Form C. 2118.

Place	Date	Hour	Summary of Events and Information	Remarks and references to Appendices
BUS	28/6/18	7 pm	Routine (8 OR [illegible]) [illegible]	
"	29/6/18	"	Routine (3 OR wnded). [illegible] shelters being taken down & rebuilt [illegible]	
"	30/6/18	"	Routine (1 off + 5 OR wnd + 1 gas wnd) Church Parades. Weather still fine.	
			[illegible signature]	

A7092. Wt W428 9/M1293 750,000. 1/17. D. D & L., Ltd. Forms/C2118/14.

WAR DIARY

OF

1/2nd EAST LANCASHIRE FIELD AMBULANCE.

FROM :- July 1st, 1918. TO :- July 31st, 1918.

(VOLUME VII)

Instructions regarding War Diaries and Intelligence Summaries are contained in F. S. Regs., Part II. and the Staff Manual respectively. Title pages will be prepared in manuscript.

WAR DIARY
or
~~INTELLIGENCE SUMMARY.~~
(Erase heading not required.)

Army Form C. 2118.

Place	Date	Hour	Summary of Events and Information	Remarks and references to Appendices
Bus.	1/7/18.		Shortly after midnight enemy planes bombed E. end of village & dropped one on billet occupied by X 42 T.M.B. wounding 17 & killing 4. Routine. Re-construction of Reception & walking wounded Room, to make it splinter proof. Wounded 21, Sick 13 of Division. Out of 87 cases (all troops) 73 Influenza cases were sent to D.R.S. The 1/10th M/c had 28 cases of Influenza & 1/5th M/c 21 cases. Weather fine & warm. CGJS	
–	2/7/18.		Raid by M/c Battalion with heavy artillery preparation. Anticipation by enemy & no prisoners taken, casualties 3 Officers & 14 O.R. mostly slight. Heavy enemy shelling of front & back areas [illegible] during most of night. Some very heavy stuff falling on [illegible] side of Bus wood. Routine. Sick of Division evacuated to D.R.S. 95 to C.C.S. 9. Wounded of Division 3 Officers & 14 O.R. Quiet day, warm & sunny. CGJ	
–	3/7/18.		Quiet night, very few cases. Routine. Visited 127th Bde Baths at COURCELLES with Col [illegible]. Two O.R. left there for duty. Wounded of Division passed thro' M.D.S. during last 24 hrs – 5 O.R. Sick 50 O.R. & 3 Officers. To D.R.S. 95 of which 80 were Influenza. Cloudy & cooler. CGJ	
	4/7/18.		V. quiet night. Routine. Pay for all ranks. Wounded of 42 Divn for last 24 hrs ~~thro~~ thro' this M.D.S. 14 O.R. To C.C.S. 3 O.R. 1 Officer. To D.R.S. 47 of which 42 were Influenza. Capt. [illegible] MORCUSA down from ~~the~~ 1/8th M/c down from the line with Influenza. CGJ	

A7092. Wt. W125 9/M1293 750,000. 1/17. D. D. & L., Ltd. Forms/C2118/14.

Instructions regarding War Diaries and Intelligence Summaries are contained in F. S. Regs., Part II. and the Staff Manual respectively. Title pages will be prepared in manuscript.

WAR DIARY

or

~~INTELLIGENCE SUMMARY.~~

(Erase heading not required.)

Army Form C. 2118.

Place	Date	Hour	Summary of Events and Information	Remarks and references to Appendices
M.D.S. BUS.	5/7/18		Heavy artillery fire in night to S.E. Routine. Visited Baths at COURCELLES AU BOIS. Three hundred men bathed & [illegible] previous day. Wounded of Division during last 24 hrs 13 O.R's. Sick to CCS 1 Officer 29 O.R's. Sixty cases sent to D.R.S. of which 51 were epidemic influenza. Weather fine. [initials]	
	6/7/18		Very quiet night indeed. Routine. Wounded of Division during last 24 hrs O.R's 6. Sick O.R's 7 to CCS. To DRS 77 OR of which 24 were epidemic influenza. Weather dull & cool. [initials]	
	7/7/18		Very quiet night. Routine. Construction work proceeding very slowly on a/c of loss of [illegible] Smith & Pte Edwards (St Valery) Wounded of Division during last 24 hrs 6 O.R's. Sick to CCS 13 O.R. 1 Officer. To DRS 79 of which 65 were influenza. Weather fine & dull at times. [initials]	
	8/7/18		Another quiet night but one case of wounds [illegible] during night. Routine. Inspection of H.T. by Major General [illegible] High commendation & [illegible] [illegible]. Gas centre in action for first [illegible] 6 cases of mustard gas treated [illegible]. Wounded of Division during last 24 hrs 7 O.R. To C.C.S. (Sick) 13 To D.R.S. 104 of which 96 were influenza. Weather fine & dull. Wonderfully quiet. Expected [illegible] [illegible] [initials]	

A7092. Wt. W12839/M1293 750,000. 1/17. D. D & L. Ltd. Forms/C2118/14.

WAR DIARY
or
~~INTELLIGENCE SUMMARY.~~
(Erase heading not required.)

Army Form C. 2118.

Instructions regarding War Diaries and Intelligence Summaries are contained in F. S. Regs., Part II. and the Staff Manual respectively. Title pages will be prepared in manuscript.

Place	Date	Hour	Summary of Events and Information	Remarks and references to Appendices
M.D.S. BUS	9/7/18		Routine. Two gas cases (6) treated at gas centre. Various improvements carried out in face of experience of last night. During last 24 hrs 82 casualties (wounded & gassed) evacuated to CCS. Sick (4) Seventy one cases sent to DRS 57 of which 55 Influenza. Showery. Capt Jones MORCUSA returns to unit from temp'y duty with AFA 293 Bde. cgw	
	10/7/18		Wet night. Routine. Visited batty at COURCELLES & found everything O.K. Commenced building of Dressing hut. Wounded of Div for last 24 hrs 14 O.R. Sick to CCS 9 O.R. To DRS 64, 44 being epidemic influenza. Very showery. cgw	
	11/7/18		Wet & quiet night. Routine. Large fatigue parties sent to help 1/131 at advance ADS. (reserve). Capt O'Driscoll returns from Temp'y duty with 1/5th M/C. Lt Sergeant returns from Leave in U.K. Sick of Division evacuated to CCS 2 O.Rs. Wounded 6 O.Rs. To DRS 54 O.Rs. 43 being influenza. Very heavy Showers. cgw.	
	12/7/18.		Routine. To C.C.S (of Division) 1 Off & 6 O.Rs sick & 9 O.Rs wounded. To DRS. 50 O.Rs including 35 O.R influenza. Very wet & muddy. Each day is a tedious repetition of the preceding one yet in all ranks is a feeling of 'Someness' & a tenacity of spirit that shows thro' the 'Sameness'. C.A.F.	

A7092 Wt W125 9/M1293 750,000. 1/17. D. D & L., Ltd. Forms/C. 2118/14.

Instructions regarding War Diaries and Intelligence Summaries are contained in F. S. Regs., Part II. and the Staff Manual respectively. Title pages will be prepared in manuscript.

WAR DIARY
or
~~INTELLIGENCE SUMMARY.~~
(*Erase heading not required.*)

Army Form C. 2118.

Place	Date	Hour	Summary of Events and Information	Remarks and references to Appendices
M.D.S BUS.	13/7/15		Routine. Divisional Sick to CCS 4 OR's wounded 3 OR' To DRS [illegible] including 40 Influenza. Showery. C.A.P.	
	14/7/15		Routine. Sick of Division to CCS 1 Off, 5 OR'. To DRS 51 including 38 Influenza. Dull & showery all day. C.A.P.	
	15/7/15		Routine. Sick of Division to CCS 5 O.R'. wounded 12 O.R'. To DRS 35 O.R' 24 only being Influenza. Capt O Dunsmore [illegible] relieved by Capt J C P Bayley & Relation 15 Cav Corps. Visited baths at COURCELLES. Weather showery early but later fine. C.A.P.	
	16/7/15		Routine. Heavy ~~thunderstorm~~ in early hours playing havoc with ~~[illegible]~~ of new Dressing Hut. Very hot day. C.O. visits Baths at COURCELLES. Sick of Division to CCS 1 Officer & 5 O.R. Wounded 14 O.R's. To DRS 74. 52 Influenza. C.A.P.	
	17/7/15		Very active ~~artillery~~ work all night. Both enemy [illegible] planes passing over ~~through~~ most of night. Routine & inspection of [illegible] BRI all [illegible]. Sick of Division to CCS 2 O.R'. wounded 2 O.R' To DRS 85 O.R of which 47 O.R Influenza. Very hot day. C.A.P.	

A5834 Wt. W4973/M687 750,000 8/16 D. D. & L. Ltd. Forms/C.2118/13.

Instructions regarding War Diaries and Intelligence Summaries are contained in F. S. Regs., Part II. and the Staff Manual respectively. Title pages will be prepared in manuscript.

WAR DIARY

or

~~INTELLIGENCE~~ SUMMARY.

(Erase heading not required.)

Army Form C. 2118.

Place	Date	Hour	Summary of Events and Information	Remarks and references to Appendices
M.D.S BUS.	18-7-18.		Routine. Capt W. H. HERR M.O.R.C. U.S.A ~~[illegible]~~ rejoined this unit from Temp'y duty with 1/3rd E.L.F.Amb. Sick of Div to CCS 1 Off. 5 O.R's. Wounded 1 Off. 26 O.R's. To DRS 7 O.R's, including 30 Influenza. Showery & Stormy. CJP	
	19/7/18		Stormy night. Bomb dropped at BERTRANCOURT & shell hit some few men of 126th B.[illegible]. Routine. Four O.R's on leave to [illegible]. Sick of Div to CCS 2 O.R. Wounded 15 O.R. The cases to DRS 36 of which 15 Influenza. Stormy [illegible] warm. CJP	
	20/7/18.		Quiet night. Routine. DDMS Corps called & inspected Camp of Gas Centre. Sick of Div to [transport] Off 1 O.R. 8 wounded – Off 2 O.R 11. To DRS 36 of which 14 were Influenza. CJP	
		5.30 p.m.	Heavy thunderstorm.	
	21/7/18.		Cloudy & rainy during greater part of night. Routine. One German P.O.W wounded, died in M.D.S. Sick of Div to CCS 3 Officers & 8 O.R's. Wounded 1 Officer & 5 O.R's. To DRS 46 O.R's of which 13 were Influenza. Weather changeable. CJP	
"	22/7/18	4/12	Routine 18 wounded other Ranks passed through M.D.S. WJM	
	23/7/18	"	Routine weather boisterous. 1 officer + 30 O.R. wounded. DJM	
	24/7/18.		Wet night. Routine. Sick of Div to CCS [illegible] O.R's. To DRS 22 O.R's including 6 Influenza. Weather cloudy [illegible]. Capt Wilson returns from leave to U.K. but being unfit to rejoin his Batt'n remains with F.A for light duty. CJP	

A5834 Wt. W4973/M687 750,000 8/16 D. D. & L. Ltd. Forms/C.2118/13.

Instructions regarding War Diaries and Intelligence Summaries are contained in F. S. Regs., Part II. and the Staff Manual respectively. Title pages will be prepared in manuscript.

WAR DIARY
or
~~INTELLIGENCE SUMMARY.~~
(Erase heading not required.)

Army Form C. 2118.

Place	Date	Hour	Summary of Events and Information	Remarks and references to Appendices
M.D.S. BUS	25/7/18		Quiet night. Capt HERRA MORCUSA detailed for temp'y duty with 1/1st E.L.F.Amb. Routine. Stormy & changeable. Visited by Staff Officers from relieving Division. Sick of Division evacuated to CCS 1 O.R. Wounded 20 O.R. Cases sent to DRS 35 O.R. of which 6 only were Influenza. [illegible]	
	26/7/18		Quiet night. Routine. Sick of Div'n to CCS 1 Off, 6 O.R. Wounded 6 O.R. To DRS 31 O.R. of which 2 were influenza. Cold & showery. [illegible]	
	27/7/18		Very quiet night not a single case of wounded all hours of darkness. Routine. Moved into new Dressing tent from operating tents. Putting finishing touches to the place. Awful weather. Heavy showers all day. Lt Col TRIST [illegible] of 2/2nd WESSEX Fd Amb & other Officers called & went round the camp etc as a preliminary to take over. Sick of Div'n to CCS 1 Officer 3 O.R. Wounded 2 O.R. To DRS 11 O.R. 4 of which were Influenza. The camp & precincts thick with mud. [illegible]	
	28/7/18		Routine. Fairly wet day. Sick of Div to CCS 2 O.R. Wounded 1 Officer and 6 O.R. To DRS 21 O.R. including 4 Influenza. [illegible]	

A7092. Wt W128 9/M1293 750,000. 1/17. D. D & L., Ltd. Forms/C2118/14.

Instructions regarding War Diaries and Intelligence Summaries are contained in F. S. Regs., Part II. and the Staff Manual respectively. Title pages will be prepared in manuscript.

WAR DIARY
or
INTELLIGENCE SUMMARY.
(*Erase heading not required.*)

Army Form C. 2118.

Place	Date	Hour	Summary of Events and Information	Remarks and references to Appendices
BUS-LES-ARTOIS.	29/7/15.		Routine. Construction of Pack Stores. Kit (clothing & boots) inspection. Sick of Div to C.C.S 1 Officer 1 O.R. Wounded nil. To D.R.S 12 including 6 Influenza. Variable weather warm at times, cloudy & showers. C.J.W.	
	30/7/15.		Routine. Sick of Div'n to C.C.S. 1 Officer 7 O.R's. Wounded 5 O.R. To D.R.S. 1 Officer & 40 O.R's of which 9 cases Influenza. Much warmer. Bright & sunny. C.J.W.	
	31/7/15.		Routine. Improving pathways etc. Sick of Div'n to C.C.S 2 O.R's. Wounded 2 O.R's. To D.R.S. 2 Officers & 30 O.R's. 6 cases of Influenza. Warm & sunny. Sports Committee organise an open air concert in evening & hot pot supper. C.J.W.	

[signature]
Lt Col
OC 1/2nd E. Lancs Field Ambulance

A7092. Wt W128 9/M1293 750,000. 1/17. D. D & L., Ltd. Forms/C2118/14.

Vol 19

140/3200.

WAR DIARY

OF

1/2nd EAST LANCASHIRE FIELD AMBULANCE.

From 1st August 1918 to 31st August 1918.

VOLUME VIII.

16

Aug. 1918

Instructions regarding War Diaries and Intelligence Summaries are contained in F. S. Regs., Part II, and the Staff Manual respectively. Title pages will be prepared in manuscript.

WAR DIARY
or
INTELLIGENCE SUMMARY.
(Erase heading not required.)

Army Form C. 2118.

Place	Date	Hour	Summary of Events and Information	Remarks and references to Appendices
M.D.S. BUS.			Much bombing by enemy machines in area during hours of darkness.	
	1/8/18		Routine. Pack-Store hut completed. Kit inspection of all O.R's. 1/Lt GIBBS MORCUSA reports for duty on returning from leave to U.K. Sick of Div to CCS 2 O.R's. Wounded 2 O.R. To DRS 24 O.R of which 5 cases of Influenza. Very hot & heavy. CGW	
	2/8/18		Heavy artillery firing heard throughout the night apparently due South. Routine. Rainy & muggy. Out door fatigues impossible. Sick of Div to CCS 1 Officer & 7 O.R. Wounded 3 O.R's. To DRS 31 O.R's including only 3 cases of Influenza. Visit by O.C. DRS Southern Area. CGW	
	3/8/18		Rainy night. Day quiet. Routine. Too wet for out door fatigues. Sick of Div'n to CCS 1 Officer & 6 O.R's. To DRS 21 O.R's including 1 case of Influenza. CGW	
	4/8/18		Routine. Sick of Div'n to CCS 2 Officers & 7 O.R's. Wounded 5 O.R's. To DRS 37 O.R's including 2 Influenza. Cricket Match in afternoon at Div Reception Camp 'Halloy'. Unit won by 4 wkts & 20 runs. Showery. Visited Baths at COURCELLES. CGW	
	5/8/18		Routine. Dull & very wet all day. Sick of Div to CCS 6 O.R's. Wounded 6 O.R's. To DRS 23 O.R's including 6 cases of Influenza. Rain demolishes one of four small dug-outs built by our predecessors. R.E's called in to examine others as to their safety. Pronounced unsafe till propped. CGW	

A7092. Wt W128 9/M1293 750,000 1/17. D. D. & L. Ltd. Forms/C2118/14.

Army Form C. 2118.

WAR DIARY
or
INTELLIGENCE SUMMARY.
(Erase heading not required.)

Instructions regarding War Diaries and Intelligence Summaries are contained in F. S. Regs., Part II. and the Staff Manual respectively. Title pages will be prepared in manuscript.

Place	Date	Hour	Summary of Events and Information	Remarks and references to Appendices
M.D.S. Bus.	6/8/18	7/p	Routine. State [illegible] inspection of Camp by a/ADMS. Sick of Div to CCS 4 O.Rs. Wounded 6 O.Rs. + DRS 39 O.Rs including 6 cases of Influenza. Gas proof [illegible] (small [illegible]) [illegible] by RE. [illegible]	
"	7/8/18	–	Routine 12 O.R. wounded WM	
"	8/8/18	–	Routine 6 O.R. wounded. Major Webster proceeded today on leave to UK. WM	
"	9/8/18	–	Routine. [illegible] 10 + 5 O.R. wounded to CCS. WM	
"	10/8/18	–	Routine 1 Off + 1 O.R. wounded. WM	
"	11/8/18	–	Routine + Church Parades. 2 wounded WM	
"	12/8/18	–	Routine. 7 wounded (one to DRS) WM. Inspection of Transport by a/OC Div Train (SSO) WM	
"	13/8/18	–	Routine. 17 O.R. wounded. A party of 2 American M.Os + 24 O.R. reported today from 80th Div. for instruction. (Major J. P. SPOONER + Capt. S. D. GLEETEN). Lieut R.H. MATHEWS MORISH reported today to this unit for duty. WM	
"	14/8/18	–	Routine. 3 O.R. wounded. Report on Transport arrived today ("Very satisfactory"). WM. 1 Sergeant + 2 O.R. American troops arrived today for instruction WM	
"	15/8/18	–	Routine. 12 O.R. wounded passed through M.D.S. during last 24 hours. [illegible] WM	
"	16/8/18	–	Routine. 2 Officers + 20 O.R. wounded. Visited COURCELLES as a possible site for M.D.S. – in view of the enemy having retired east of SERRES. WM	
"	17/8/18	–	Routine. 10 + 17 O.R. wounded WM	
"	18/8/18	–	Routine 18 O.R. wounded WM	
"	19/8/18	–	Routine 10 + 15 O.R. wounded.	

A7092. Wt. W128 9/M1293 750,000. 1/17. D. D. & L., Ltd. Forms/C2118/14.

WAR DIARY
or
INTELLIGENCE SUMMARY.
(*Erase heading not required.*)

Army Form C. 2118.

Instructions regarding War Diaries and Intelligence Summaries are contained in F. S. Regs., Part II. and the Staff Manual respectively. Title pages will be prepared in manuscript.

Place	Date	Hour	Summary of Events and Information	Remarks and references to Appendices
MDS BUS	20/8/18	7pm	Routine: 11 OR wounded passed through MDS. WTM	
	21/8/18	"	British attacked this morning the 21st Division between Beaumont Hamel + Puisieux. Up to 12 noon the total through the MDS was 1 officer + [illegible] 3 German soldiers. All the lying cases came to ADS from Courcelles ADS. The walking wounded were arranged for Courcelles to Louvencourt by lorries. Casualties evidently comparatively few. WTM D.D.G.M.S. visited MDS & expressed satisfaction. WTM	
"	22/8/18	"	4 officers + 79 OR British wounded (including about 8 gas cases) passed through MDS. Also 2 off + 8 OR German wounded. Two of the German cases were [illegible]. One was however in articulo when he arrived & later died. Capt Neame transfused one badly wounded man, the donor being Pte BOARDMAN (352391). The patient was improved markedly. DMS Third Army visited MDS & expressed satisfaction. WTM The officers here at present are Self, Major PURVES, Capt GIBSON, Capt NEAME, Lieut MATHEWS, MORCUSA. Capt HERR proceeded for temporary duty to the 5th Manchesters. Lieut GIBBS is with the 8th Manchesters. Major Webster on leave & Quartermaster & Lieut LOWE is with the unit. WTM	
"	23/8/18	"	3 officers + 127 OR + 3 OR German wounded passed through MDS. Evacuation working smoothly. The MAC cars worked at MDS from 5 to 7. Capt NEAME proceeded on leave to U.K. today.	

Instructions regarding War Diaries and Intelligence Summaries are contained in F. S. Regs., Part II. and the Staff Manual respectively. Title pages will be prepared in manuscript.

WAR DIARY
or
INTELLIGENCE SUMMARY.
(Erase heading not required.)

Army Form C. 2118.

Place	Date	Hour	Summary of Events and Information	Remarks and references to Appendices
~~24/8/18~~	~~7pm~~		Routine. 1 officer + 29 OR + 3 German wounded passed through. Weather fine.	
BUS	24/8/18	7pm	The Field Ambulance moved here last night, took over the ADS buildings from the 1/1st FA & formed a MDS, leaving a guard of two men on the old site. The line having advanced beyond Miraumont, arrangements are being made to form an MDS there.	
COURCELLES au-BOIS	25/8/18	"	2 officers + 72 OR British passed through wounded + 18 OR German. Arrangements working smoothly. PM. Capt Delafield & Lieut White of 3rd FA reported for duty.	
MIRAUMONT	26/8/18	"	MDS opened at MIRAUMONT with 1 tent subdivision. HQ of unit moved also. Opened at 6pm. Capt Delafield sent to PUISIEUX to form Walking Wounded Collecting Station, with 2 sergeants & 40 R. Later a party of about 20 OR 3rd FA reported to him for duty. At the MDS are Capt [illegible], Lieut Mathews, Lieut White & self. 93 OR passed through MDS & 3 P.O.W. during last 24 hours. [illegible]	
"	27/8/18	"	2 officers + 71 OR + 2 POW passed through MDS. Remainder of tent subdivision arrived today at MIRAUMONT. (Map reference L.35 C.8.5).	
	28/8/18	"	Routine. Personnel employed [illegible] for MDS [illegible]. Lying cases sent to CCS GEZAINCOURT, walking wounded by lorry to PUISIEUX Rly Station. [illegible] to DRS LOUVENCOURT. 15 OR British + 2 OR German wounded. [illegible]	
	29/8/18	"	Routine. 1 officer + 35 OR wounded. Preparations being made to move to LE BARQUE.	

A7092. Wt W128 9/M1293 750,000 1/17. D. D & L., Ltd. Forms/C2118/14.

Instructions regarding War Diaries and Intelligence Summaries are contained in F. S. Regs., Part II. and the Staff Manual respectively. Title pages will be prepared in manuscript.

WAR DIARY
or
INTELLIGENCE SUMMARY.

(Erase heading not required.)

Army Form C. 2118.

Place	Date	Hour	Summary of Events and Information	Remarks and references to Appendices
PYS	Aug 30/18	7/m	Visits LE BARQUE at 6 am & find it unsuitable for MDS very dirty & area usually shelled rather heavily. Selected spot at East end of village of PYS (M.d.o.2) where MDS was opened at 12 midday. Remainder of ambulance ready in by 6 pm. MIRAUMONT was cleared by H.Q. Today there were 30 + 106 OR passed through MDS. [illegible] site in the village WM.	
"	Aug 31/18		Routine. MDS rather busier during last 24 hours. 70 + 181 OR British + 11 POW. MDS shelled this afternoon chiefly by Gas shells no casualties in the unit [illegible]	

A7092 Wt W128 9/M1293 750,000 1/17 D. D. & L., Ltd. Forms/C2118/14.

WAR DIARY

OF

1/2nd EAST LANCASHIRE FIELD AMBULANCE.

September 1st 1918 to September 30th 1918.

VOLUME IX.

Army Form C. 2118.

Instructions regarding War Diaries and Intelligence Summaries are contained in F. S. Regs., Part II. and the Staff Manual respectively. Title pages will be prepared in manuscript.

WAR DIARY
or
INTELLIGENCE SUMMARY.

(Erase heading not required.)

Place	Date	Hour	Summary of Events and Information	Remarks and references to Appendices
P.Y.S	1/IX/18	7pm	Owing to site of MDS being shelled yesterday three times the MDS was moved to side of a ? road (to LESARS) about 300 yds further S.W. where there is excellent amount of cover from a high bank. 5 officers + 87 OR + 4 POW wounded passed through MDS. Weather fine. WM	
"	2/IX/18	"	No hostile shelling of area past MDS. 5 officers + 39 OR + 3 POW wounded. Today with ADMS I visited area past LE BARQUE with view to locating MDS there. WM	
M.12a.~~58~~ 39	3/IX/18	"	MDS moved to M.12.a.5.8 on Bapaume - Albert road. 6 officers + 140 OR + 67 POW passed through MDS. Visited BARASTRE with ADMS with view to advancing MDS there. WM	
N.18 b.5.8	4/IX/18	"	MDS opened near VILLERS-au-FLOS at 9am all transport brought up later. Dump of ? plus material left in charge of 3 OR at M.12.a.5.8. 1 O + 38 OR + 5 POW passed through.	
"	5/IX/18	"	4 officers + 78 OR + 1 POW wounded passed through MDS. Capt HERN proceeded to 5/East Lancs Regt as MO i/c temporarily. WM	
M.12.a.3.9.	6/IX/18	"	Unit moved today from N.18.b.5.8. back to M.12.a.3.9. the site a few days ago, the division having gone into Corps Reserve. 5 officers + 58 OR + 11 POW wounded through MDS.	
"	7/IX/18	"	Routine. No wounded passed through MDS. Inspecting clothing equipment + SBRs ? WM	
"	8/IX/18	"	Church Parades. Various fatigues. 1 officer + 1 OR wounded. WM	
"	9/IX/18	"	Routine. WM	
"	10/IX/18	"	Routine. Cleaning stores & equipment. WM	
"	11/IX/18	"	Routine. WM	

A7092. Wt W128 9/M1293 750,000. 1/17. D. D. & L., Ltd. Forms/C2118/14.

Instructions regarding War Diaries and Intelligence Summaries are contained in F. S. Regs., Part II. and the Staff Manual respectively. Title pages will be prepared in manuscript.

WAR DIARY
or
INTELLIGENCE SUMMARY.
(Erase heading not required.)

Army Form C. 2118.

Place	Date	Hour	Summary of Events and Information	Remarks and references to Appendices
Mazières [illegible]	12/9/18	7/14	Routine. WTM	
"	13/9/18	"	Routine. Route marching. WTM	
"	14/9/18		Routine – Gas Respirators inspected & drill. Capt GIBSON proceeded to UK on leave. Lieut MATHEWS proceeded to 56 CCS for temporary duty [illegible]	
"	15/9/18	"	Routine: Church Parades. WTM	
"	16/9/18	"	Routine WTM Major Webster returns from leave WTM	
"	17/9/18	"	Routine. Thanks [illegible] the use of the Thresh Disinfector – all our blankets were disinfected [illegible]	
"	18/9/18	"	Routine. Construction of Bomb protection for Horses. Major Webster & I proceeded to YTRES in connection with Defence Scheme. WTM	
"	19/9/18	"	Routine, Visits RUYAULCOURT & HAVRINCOURT Wood in view of relieving 50th [illegible] 37th Div. on the 21st WTM	
"	20/9/18	"	Routine. Capt Nearne & about 20 O.R. proceeded [illegible] to Havrincourt Wood to relieve a corresponding number of the 50th FA (37th Div) Arrangements being made to complete relief tomorrow of the ADS at RUYAULCOURT. WTM	
Ruyaulcourt	21/9/18	"	Field Ambulance moved today to Ruyaulcourt & relieved 50th FA at ADS, bearer posts &c. About 20 bearers & Major Haskins MC reported for duty last night with the unit. Also Two Daimler Cars & one Ford from 3rd FA. One motor cycle from 1st FA [illegible] MDS is at LEBUCQUIERE run by 1st FA. Our personnel are dotted in dugouts. A Nissen hut is used as ADS. WTM	
"	22/9/18	"	Visited forward area with Major Haskins MC. WTM	
"	23/9/18	"	Major Webster & Major Haskins visits forward area today. About 150 Gas Cases passed through ADS these last two days. WTM	
"	24/9/18		Conference at ADMS office. Lieut LOWE proceeded on leave today. WTM	

Instructions regarding War Diaries and Intelligence Summaries are contained in F. S. Regs., Part II. and the Staff Manual respectively. Title pages will be prepared in manuscript.

WAR DIARY
or
INTELLIGENCE SUMMARY.

(Erase heading not required.)

Army Form C. 2118.

Place	Date	Hour	Summary of Events and Information	Remarks and references to Appendices
Royaulcourt	25/9/18	7pm	Routine visits L R.A.P. & Centre R.A.P. with Major Haskins M.C. today. Evacuation from line proceeding satisfactorily. WTm	
"	26/9/18	"	[illegible] of [illegible] Bearers of [illegible] A B report [illegible] Major [illegible] & proceeded to Clayton Cross [illegible] Post. WTm	
"	27/9/18	"	British attack on extended front: Casualties Evacuation in good order	
"	28/9/18	"	A.D.S. formed at Q 15.a.6.3. Officers at A.D.S. Major [illegible] Lieut Douglas M.O.R.C.U.S.A. who has been with the unit for two days detailed for duty [illegible] 42 [illegible] Capt [illegible] & Major Haskins M.C.	
"	29/9/18	"	The Division was relieved by N.Z. Div. our old site – Royaulcourt was taken over by a N.Z. Fd Amb as M.D.S. Our A.D.S. – Q 15.a.6.3 remains [illegible] [illegible] of division. The bearers have returned [illegible] except the [illegible] attached to each battalion & the Brigade [illegible] Clayton Cross is held as a [illegible] place [illegible] the Batt [illegible] S.B.s about 100 in number. WTm	
	30/9/18	"	~~Instructions~~ given to Batt M.O.s ~~[illegible]~~ to return to unit the R.A.M.C. [illegible] Lieut Douglas M.O.R.C.U.S.A. proceeded for duty to 5th Manchesters relieving Lieut [illegible]	

[signature]

Lieut. Col. R.A.M.C. (T.)

O.C. ½ East Lancs. Field Ambulance.

A7092. Wt. W128 9/M1293 750,000. 1/17. D. D & L. Ltd. Forms/C2118/14.

WAR DIARY

OF

1/2nd EAST LANCASHIRE FIELD AMBULANCE.

October 1st 1918 to October 31st 1918.

VOLUME X.

Army Form C. 2118.

Instructions regarding War Diaries and Intelligence Summaries are contained in F. S. Regs., Part II. and the Staff Manual respectively. Title pages will be prepared in manuscript.

WAR DIARY
or
INTELLIGENCE SUMMARY.
(Erase heading not required.)

Place	Date	Hour	Summary of Events and Information	Remarks and references to Appendices
Royalcourt	1918 Oct 1	7 pm	Routine. men being [illegible] + bathed W.M.	
RUYALCOURT	Oct 2	7 pm	Routine W.J.P	
"	Oct 3	7 pm	Routine W.J.P	
"	Oct 4	7 pm	Routine, Lieut-Col. MUNRO M.C. on leave, Major W.J. PURVES MC took over Temporary Command W.J.P	
"	" 5	7 pm	Routine. G.O.C 42 Div. inspected the Camp, also Transport accompanied by A.D.M.S. W.J.P	
"	" 6	7 pm	Routine. W.J.P	
"	" 7	7 pm	Visited forward area along with ADMS, called on No 1 New Zealand Fd Amb. A.D.S at G. 32. A. 8. 7. + Car Post at G 32 D 2.8. MAJOR C.A. WEBSTER returned to Hdqrs. W.J.P	Map Ref 57.B. 1.40000
RIBECOURT	" 8	7 pm	This Fd Amb with Headquarters at RUYAULCOURT P. 10 A 8. 4. + detached Section at Q 15 A 7. 4. (Map Ref. 57C 1.40 000) moved to RIBECOURT where the Headquarters was opened, and an advanced Section took over a post from No 1 New Zealand Fd Amb at G. 32. D 2. 8. Map Ref 57B in preparation of going forward. Officers at this advanced post are Capt NEAME + Capt. GIBSON, MAJOR WEBSTER acting second in command was stationed at Hdqrs W.J.P	Map Ref 57.C 1.40000
LESDAIN	" 9	1900.	Capt NEAME moved with A.D.S. personnel to LESDAIN H. 31. C 7. 3, remainder of officers + personnel moved from RIBECOURT to LESDAIN, transport also. Capt. NEAME + Capt GIBSON with ADS personnel moved forward again at 2 P.M. to ESNES H 34 D. 1. 7. Headquarters was established there at 7 P.M.	Map Ref 57. B. 57. B

A7092. Wt. W.128 g/M1293 750,000. 1/17. D. D & L., Ltd. Forms/C2118/14.

Instructions regarding War Diaries and Intelligence Summaries are contained in F. S. Regs., Part II. and the Staff Manual respectively. Title pages will be prepared in manuscript.

WAR DIARY
or
INTELLIGENCE SUMMARY.
(Erase heading not required.)

Army Form C. 2118.

Place	Date	Hour	Summary of Events and Information	Remarks and references to Appendices
LESDAIN	Oct 9	1900	One officer MAJOR JOHNSTONE M.C & 37 O.R. bearers arrived for duty. WOUNDED. 42 DIV - 10. Sick Three. " N.Z. DIV. NIL " one. WOUNDED 37 DIV 3. NIL " German 1 NIL W/P.	Map Ref 57. B
ESNES	10	1900	Roads to BEAUVOIS-EN-CAMBRAI were reconnoitred, several cross roads had been blown up. MAJOR WEBSTER & personnel, & TRANSPORT moved from LESDAIN at 1400. MAJOR WEBSTER & personnel, & TRANSPORT moved from LESDAIN at 1400. MAJOR JOHNSTONE M.C. & his bearers to ESNES, also MAJOR JOHNSTONE M.C. & his bearers. Officers at ESNES at 1900 MAJOR PURVES RCC. MAJOR WEBSTER. CAPT NEAME, CAPT GIBSON, CAPT HERR. U.S.A MAJOR JOHNSTONE MC. ADMS instructed that this UNIT would collect the WOUNDED from of the three BRIGADES, 126, 125 & 127. W/P	
BEAUVOIS	11	1900	Capt. NEAME Capt GIBSON along with the personnel of the advanced A.D.S. left ESNES & moved to JEUNE BOIS BREWERY I XI D 5.9. & established an A.D.S. MAJOR WEBSTER, MAJOR JOHNSTONE MC CAPT HERR U.S.A brought the remainder of personnel & Transport. Self & Capt NEAME visited VIESLY D 28 & marked a place for an A.D.S Fifty bearers reported from 1/1 E.L Fd Amb. Wounded NIL, SICK 42 DIV 5. W/P	Map Ref 57. B 57. B

A5834 Wt. W4973/M687 750,000 8/16 D. D. & L. Ltd. Forms/C.2118/13.

WAR DIARY
or
INTELLIGENCE SUMMARY.
(*Erase heading not required.*)

Army Form C. 2118.

Instructions regarding War Diaries and Intelligence Summaries are contained in F. S. Regs., Part II. and the Staff Manual respectively. Title pages will be prepared in manuscript.

Place	Date	Hour	Summary of Events and Information	Remarks and references to Appendices
BEAUVOIS	Oct./18 12	1900	CAPT NEAME & Capt GIBSON along with 50 O.R. moved to VIESLY & established A.D.S. at D 28 C 8.2. (Map Ref 57 B) good cellar cover. Transport - 2 A.D.S. limbers, one Water Cart, Two Ford Cars. evacuation from A.D.S. to JEUNEBOIS in Ford Car, then from JEUNE BOIS to M.D.S. at SUCERIE H.18.D.0.8. Reserve Bearer post established at PREYELLE J.3C.2.2. personnel there MAJOR JOHNSTONE M.C. and 55 bearers. Transport One Daimler Car, ~~Stretchers & Blankets~~ One Water Cart. Stretchers & Blankets.	57.B. W/P
BEAUVOIS	13th	1900	R.A.P. established at D 28. C 6, 9, 1/8 LANC Fus^s (left front) D 28 A 9.0. 1/5 LANC. Fus^s (Rt front) D 26. A 8.8, 1/7 LANC Fus^s left ~~support~~ Batt. D 26 D 8.3, 1/8 MANCH Rt. support MAJOR JOHNSTONE M.C returned to JEUNE BOIS, Thirty more bearers reported to Capt NEAME. Considered the reserve bearer post at PREYELLE unsafe, & the distance between JEUNE BOIS and VIESLY is easily covered in case of emergency. MAJOR JOHNSTONE M.C established a bearer relay post, & walking wounded post at HERPIGNY FARM. D 25 d 2.7. 1 N.C.O. and 8 men, also Horse AMB at AULICOURT FARM J.1. a central, 2 3 quads Capt NEAME arranged & organised the removal of several old civilians from BRIASTRE E 24 & 30. They were unable to walk, the town heavily shelled	57.B W/P W/P

A5834 Wt. W4973/M687 750,000 8/16 D. D. & L. Ltd. Forms/C.2118/13.

Instructions regarding War Diaries and Intelligence Summaries are contained in F. S. Regs., Part II. and the Staff Manual respectively. Title pages will be prepared in manuscript.

WAR DIARY
or
INTELLIGENCE SUMMARY.
(Erase heading not required.)

Army Form C. 2118.

Place	Date	Hour	Summary of Events and Information	Remarks and references to Appendices
BEAUVOIS	Oct 14	1900	Visited A.D.S. enemy are shelling the centre of VIESLY. 1/8 L.F. changed R.A.P. from D28 c 6.9. to D28 d 8.7. Relay Post was established at HERPIGNY FARM D25, d, 2.7. Routes of Evacuation:— 1/5 Lanc Fus. D28 a 9.0 } By wheeled Stretcher to ADS VIESLY D28 c 8.2 1/8 " " D28 a 8.7 } (2 Fords + 1 Daimler Stationed at ADS) 1/7 Lanc Fus. D26 a 8.8 (Support Bn) Wheeled Stretcher to Relay Post 1/8th Manch Rgt. D26 d 8.3 (" ") at HERPIGNY FARM D25 d 2.4 Horse Ambulance at AULICOURT FARM J.1.a Central attached to 126th Inf Brigade HQ Stretcher Cases from HERPIGNY + AULICOURT FARMS + ADS by Car to JEUNNE BOIS. Walking in ambulance across country to JEUNNE BOIS. W/P	Maps Ref. 57. B
BEAUVOIS	15	1900	Visited ADS R.A.P.s 1/8 L.F, 1/5 L.F, 1/8 M. also Relay Post at HERPIGNY FARM. French medical man called + informed us that the Germans had many cases of Dysentery stationed in JEUNE BOIS, average number of deaths 6 per day; Reported that BEVILLERS AREA was the worst for Dysentery. WATER is being examined, awaiting report. Buildings + quarters are all being well disinfected Capt NEAME organised another party + removed 20 more remaining civilians from BRIASTRE D24.c 8.0. W/P	57. B

A5834 Wt W4973/M687 750,000 8/16 D. D. & L. Ltd. Forms/C.2118/13.

Instructions regarding War Diaries and Intelligence Summaries are contained in F. S. Regs., Part II. and the Staff Manual respectively. Title pages will be prepared in manuscript.

WAR DIARY
or
INTELLIGENCE SUMMARY.
(Erase heading not required.)

Army Form C. 2118.

Place	Date	Hour	Summary of Events and Information	Remarks and references to Appendices
BEAUVOIS	Oct. 16	1900	Visited A.D.S. 1/7 LANCS FUS: took over from 1/8 LANCS FUS: M.O.s exchanged R.A.P.s Disinfected the buildings with Cresol solution, & whitewashed, to prevent any possible spread of Dysentery. W.P.	Maps Ref 57B NE 1:20000
BEAUVOIS	17th	1900	Visited A.D.S. VIESLY was shelled in the early hours, no casualties, one water cart, one Sawyers Stove damaged by shell fire. Arrangements completed for handling many stretcher cases, & walking wounded, also separate place for G.A.S. cases. LIEUT. GIBBS MORCUSA taken on the strength. W.P.	
BEAUVOIS	18th	1900	Visited A.D.S. Headquarters, Car stand, & Horse Amb: stand fixed & arranged. for at PRAYELLE J2 d. 8.3. all stretchers & blankets at A.D.S. L/Corp: Hodgson R. of this unit was wounded, Comp: fracture left thigh. Capt HERR MORCUSA detailed for temporary duty with 42 Div. Reception Camp. 126 Bde relieved the 125 Bde, 1/8 LANCS FUS: attached 126 Bde. W.P.	
BEAUVOIS	19th	1900	Visited A.D.S. Officers CAPT NEAME, CAPT GIBSON, LIEUT GIBBS MORCUSA MAJOR JOHNSTONE M.C. attached from 1/3 E.L. Fd Amb. A.D.S. MAJOR PURVES, MAJOR WEBSTER. PRAYELLE. LIEUT-Col. W.F. MUNRO M.C. returned from leave 2 Officers & 100 stretcher bearers reported for duty from the BATTLE Surplus. W.P.	

A5834 Wt. W4973/M687 750,000 8/16 D. D. & L. Ltd. Forms/C.2118/13.

Instructions regarding War Diaries and Intelligence Summaries are contained in F. S. Regs., Part II. and the Staff Manual respectively. Title pages will be prepared in manuscript.

WAR DIARY
or
INTELLIGENCE SUMMARY.
(Erase heading not required.)

Army Form C. 2118.

Place	Date	Hour	Summary of Events and Information	Remarks and references to Appendices
PRAYELLE	20/10/18	7 pm	HQ moved to PRAYELLE which was used as a Car Post, on BETHENCOURT–VIESLY Road. Transport (HT) & QM Department remained at JEUNE BOIS. In the morning the Division attacked & noticeably in the afternoon the ADS was moved to village of BRIASTRE from VIESLY. About 115 lying & 227 walking British wounded passed through our hands. & about 33 lying & 30 walking P.O.W. also. Wm	
VIESLY	21/10/18	"	HQ moved to VIESLEY as well as all transport & QM department from JEUNE BOIS. Weather wet. Wm	
"	22/10/18	"	Arranging routes of Evacuation & Bearer Posts also arranging work of ADS at BRIASTRE	
"	23/10/18	"	125th Brigade attacked this morning. Collecting & evacuation of wounded satisfactorily accomplished. Approximately 160 patients passed through our hands on this occasion very few of whom were lying cases & very few prisoners. At 10.40 am the New Zealand Medical Service opened an MDS at VIESLEY their division having previously gone through our division and our Divisional MDS at JEUNE BOIS closed. Later on the RAMC bearers returned to HQ & the ADS Briastre was closed. About 100 blankets & 150 stretchers were handed over to N.Z Field Ambulance, & to 37th Division. In the evening our Motor ambulances were called on to help in clearing the MDS (New Zealand) as the MAC Cars had to carry cases to YTRES. The ADS party returned to HQ at VIESLEY. Wm	
BEAUVOIS	24/10/18	"	To day the Field Ambulance moved to I16a4.4. BEAUVOIS where good buildings were. The Motor & Horse Ambulances of the other three ambulances were sent back Wm	

A5834 Wt. W4973/M687 750,000 8/16 D. D. & L. Ltd. Forms/C.2118/13.

Instructions regarding War Diaries and Intelligence Summaries are contained in F. S. Regs., Part II. and the Staff Manual respectively. Title pages will be prepared in manuscript.

WAR DIARY
or
INTELLIGENCE SUMMARY.

(Erase heading not required.)

Army Form C. 2118.

Place	Date	Hour	Summary of Events and Information	Remarks and references to Appendices
Beauvois Contd.	24/10/18	7pm	to their respective units as well as ~~their personnel~~	
"	25/10/18	–	Personnel much refreshed, having had good billets. Engaged chiefly in cleaning up kits & equipment wagons &c. Capt HERR, MORCUSA & Lieut MATTHEWS MORCUSA returned for duty today, the first from Div. reception camp, the latter from C.C.S. Capt GIBSON temporarily attached to 1/5 Lan Fusiliers as M.O. i/c. The other officers here are Major PURVES, M.C. Major WEBSTER Capt NEAME & Lieut LOWE, as well as Lieut GIBBS MORCUSA. Collection of 125 & 127th Inf Bn MG Battalion performed today. Cases sent either to DRS which is now in CAUDRY or to CCS STRES. WTM	
"	26/10/18	–	Routine. Cleaning up. Pay. WTM.	
"	27/10/18	–	Baths for personnel. Recreation (Sunday) WTM	
"	28/10/18	–	Routine. WTM.	
"	29/10/18	–	Routine. Clearing up area. Removal of manure & rubbish left by the Germans to manure dumps. WTM	
"	30/10/18	–	Routine. Foot Parades daily. WTM.	
"	31/10/18	–	Routine. Inspection of Horse Transport by O.C. Div. Train	

W. [illegible] Lt Col
OC 1/2 E Lancs Fd Amb

A5834 Wt. W4973/M687 750,000 8/16 D. D. & L. Ltd. Forms/C.2118/13.

WAR DIARY

OF

1/2nd EAST LANCASHIRE FIELD AMBULANCE

FROM :- November 1st, 1918 TO :- November 30th, 1918.

(VOLUME XI)

Instructions regarding War Diaries and Intelligence Summaries are contained in F. S. Regs., Part II. and the Staff Manual respectively. Title pages will be prepared in manuscript.

WAR DIARY
or
INTELLIGENCE SUMMARY.
(*Erase heading not required.*)

Army Form C. 2118.

Place	Date	Hour	Summary of Events and Information	Remarks and references to Appendices
BEAUVOIS	Nov 1/18	7 pm	Routine. WM	
1/6 2/14	2/18	"	Routine Baths for personnel. WM	
57 B [illegible]	3/18	"	Loading transport wagons preparatory to move. Visit to new M.D.S. Conference of 7th [illegible] at A.D.M.S. office. Report for O.C. Train re H.T. [illegible] Report called. WM Bearers attached to units of 126 Bde WM	
SOLESMES	4/18	"	Unit moved today to SOLESMES. WM	
BEAUDIGNIES	5/18	"	Unit moved to Beaudignies today. Took over MDS at 10 pm from N Z Div. WM	
LE QUESNOY	6/18	"	Unit moved to LE QUESNOY today. Opened MDS at 12 midday at old German Hospital Site. Despatched bearers to A DS + 2 Daimler Cars WM.	
"	7/18	"	Capt Hutchinson RAMC (TC) reported for temporary duty from M.G. Battn. Sick 2 Off + 34 OR + 12 POW passed ~~through~~ our hands. WM. Wounded 8 Off + 160 OR. Visited MDS today. WM.	
"	8/18	"	Advanced MDS opened at MAISON ROUGE. Major Webber & Capt Neame there. Visited HARGNIES with Capt Neame & fixed on suitable site for M.D.S. 34 OR sick — 5 officers + 59 O.R. passed through our hands today WM	
MAISON ROUGE	9/18	"	With the exception of HT (which is still at LE QUESNOY) all the unit moved here today. Few wounded now passing through. Road very bad for Motor traffic. WM 1 Off + 70 OR wounded + 4 Officers + 15 Sick. WM	

Instructions regarding War Diaries and Intelligence Summaries are contained in F. S. Regs., Part II. and the Staff Manual respectively. Title pages will be prepared in manuscript.

WAR DIARY
or
INTELLIGENCE SUMMARY.
(Erase heading not required.)

Army Form C. 2118.

Place	Date	Hour	Summary of Events and Information	Remarks and references to Appendices
MAISON ROUGE	10/11/18	7/12	Routine. Site selected at HAUTMONT for MDS & Capt [illegible] & Capt Hutchinson with personnel [illegible] & 8 MAC cars despatched there [illegible] [illegible] at 12 midnight. WM. Sick 1 officer + 30 OR, wounded 2 officers + 29 OR passed through MDS. These include 1 officer + 10 OR wounded & 15 OR sick including British, American, Italian & Russian prisoners of war. 6 civilians wounded. WM	
HAUTMONT	11/11/18	7/12	MDS moved to-day to HAUTMONT. Roads very heavy. WM. ARMISTICE at 1100 hrs.	
"	12/11/18	"	Routine. Sick of 126 Brigade collected. The unit is accommodated in ECOLE COMMUNALE. WM	
"	13/11/18	"	Routine. Remainder of Transport (G.S. wagons + 1 water cart) came today from MAISON ROUGE. WM.	
"	14/11/18	"	Routine. Kit & clothing inspection. WM	
"	15/11/18	"	Routine. Evacuation of cases to CCS for [illegible] 1st & 2nd FA. WM	
"	16/11/18	"	Routine. WM. Capt Gibson returned to duty yesterday from 1/7 L. Fusiliers WM	
"	17/11/18	"	Routine. Church Parade. WM. MAC cars removed. All sick [illegible] Div [illegible] WM	
"	18/11/18	—	Routine. WM	
"	19/11/18	"	Routine. Personnel paid. WM. Capt Gibson acting as [illegible] Demobilization & Education Officer WM	
"	20/11/18		Routine. [illegible] (about 30 patients) [illegible] 2nd FA who have not come to Hautmont. Repat- [illegible] WM	

Instructions regarding War Diaries and Intelligence Summaries are contained in F. S. Regs., Part II. and the Staff Manual respectively. Title pages will be prepared in manuscript.

WAR DIARY
or
INTELLIGENCE SUMMARY.
(Erase heading not required.)

Army Form C. 2118.

Place	Date	Hour	Summary of Events and Information	Remarks and references to Appendices
HAUTMONT	21/XI/18	7/m	Routine. Inspection of H.T. by D.A.D.V.S. WM –	
"	22/XI/18	"	Routine WM	
"	23/XI/18	"	Routine. Lieut Carroll P. reported ~~this~~ Evening for duty. All cars out of action except 1 Daimler & 1 Ford with H.D.M.S.	
"	24/XI/18	–	Church Parades. WM –	
"	25/XI/18	"	Routine. WM	
"	26/XI/18	"	Routine. WM	
"	27/XI/18	–	Routine. WM	
"	28/XI/18	–	Routine. weather wet. WM.	
"	30/XI/18	–	Routine. At present we have two Ford ambulances & one Daimler fit to take the road the others are either in workshop lads or have been evacuated. Sick rate lessening WM.	

W. D. Munro
Lieut. Col. R.A.M.C. (T.)
O.C. 1/3 East Lancs. Field Ambulance.

A5834 Wt. W4973/M687 750,000 8/16 D. D. & L. Ltd. Forms/C.2118/13.

WO 95/2923 140/5481

Confidential

WAR DIARY

OF

1/2nd EAST LANCASHIRE FIELD AMBULANCE

FROM :- DECEMBER 1st 1918 **TO** :- DECEMBER 31st 1918.

(VOLUME XII)

17

Dec. 1918

Instructions regarding War Diaries and Intelligence Summaries are contained in F. S. Regs., Part II. and the Staff Manual respectively. Title pages will be prepared in manuscript.

WAR DIARY
or
INTELLIGENCE SUMMARY.
(Erase heading not required.)

Army Form C. 2118.

Place	Date	Hour	Summary of Events and Information	Remarks and references to Appendices
HAUTMONT	Decr 1/12/18	7pm	H. M. The King passed along the MAUBEUGE – AVESNES Road this forenoon. The unit paraded & lined part of the road. All available officers & men present.	
"	2/12	"	Routine. The first lesson of the Commercial Class took place this morning. A Commercial Class & a Technical Class have been formed. Each holds three lessons per week. Capt Gibson is the unit Education officer as well as Demobilization officer. The following are the officers of the unit: The C.O. Major Purves M.C. Major [illegible] Capt Gibson Capt Hearne. Lieut CARROLL & Lieut LOWE. Lieut Matthews MORCUSA has been posted [illegible] to the 1/7th [illegible] Regt. Cars available are 1 Daimler 1 Sunbeam 2 Fords. The other 3 Daimlers are in hands of workshop. DHM.	
"	3/12/18	"	Routine — weather wet DHM	
"	4/12/18	"	Routine. Lieut CARROLL with 10 O.R. proceeded to No 5 CCS SOUS-LE-BOIS for duty. DHM.	
"	5/12/18	"	Routine. DHM.	
"	6/12/18	"	Routine. Visited Charleroi (CHARLEROI) & met ADMS to view site for DRS.	
"	7/12/18	"	Routine. Inspected ambulance today; was in full working order. DHM.	

A7092). Wt. W12839/M1293 750,000. 1/17. D. D & L., Ltd. Forms/C2118/14.

Instructions regarding War Diaries and Intelligence Summaries are contained in F. S. Regs., Part II. and the Staff Manual respectively. Title pages will be prepared in manuscript.

WAR DIARY
or
INTELLIGENCE SUMMARY.
(Erase heading not required.)

Army Form C. 2118.

Place	Date	Hour	Summary of Events and Information	Remarks and references to Appendices
HAUTMONT	Dec 8/18	7 pm	Routine & Church Parades. WTM	
	Dec 9/18	"	Routine — A further two Sunbeam motor ambulances & all drivers reported for duty with this unit to-day.	
"	Dec 10/18	"	Routine: Major PURVES MC & adj ordered to report at Adastral House London, presumably for demobilization. Handed over Imprest account to Major Webster who is now the Senior officer & the Canteen funds in Lieut Lowe's charge remain with that officer, Major Webster having desired this. Weather wet. WTM	
			[illegible signature] Lieut Col. RAMC(T)	
	11/12/18		Lt Col WT Munro MC & Major Purves MC left for England acting on orders received from W.O. Command of unit taken over by Major C H Webster. Routine — CHW	
	12/12/18		Routine — Orders for move to CHARLEROI area rec'd & preliminary preparations for same made. CHW	

Army Form C. 2118.

Instructions regarding War Diaries and Intelligence Summaries are contained in F. S. Regs., Part II. and the Staff Manual respectively. Title pages will be prepared in manuscript.

WAR DIARY
or
INTELLIGENCE SUMMARY.
(Erase heading not required.)

Place	Date	Hour	Summary of Events and Information	Remarks and references to Appendices
GRAND RENG (BELGIUM)	Dec 14	7 pm	Field Ambulance moved from HAUTMONT at 9 am along with 126 Inf Brigade to GRAND RENG arrived at 2pm. Personnel accomodated in Civilian Billets. Picked up on March 34 O.R. Capt H Neame returned to Field Amb from Temp duty with 210 Bdge R.F.A. CW	
BINCHE (Belgium)	Dec 15	7 pm	Moved from GRAND RENG along with 126 Inf Brigade at 9 am arrived BINCHE 1.30pm picked up on March 28 O.R. Personnel accomodated in Civilian Billets CW	
FONTAINE L'EVEQUE	Dec 16	4 pm	Moved from BINCHE at 9.30 am along with 126 Inf Brigade arrived FONTAINE L'EVEQUE 1.30 pm one man of the Brigade fell out on the march. Personnel accomodated in civilian Billets weather variable CW	
"	Dec 17	4 pm	Routine. Personnel Paid. Weather variable. Transport cleaned & oiled. MONTIGNY-SUR-SAMBRE reconnoitred by Capt H Neame for billets CW	

A7092). Wt. W12839/M1293 750,000. 1/17. D. D & L., Ltd. Forms/C2118/14.

Army Form C. 2118.

WAR DIARY
or
INTELLIGENCE SUMMARY.
(Erase heading not required.)

Instructions regarding War Diaries and Intelligence Summaries are contained in F. S. Regs., Part II. and the Staff Manual respectively. Title pages will be prepared in manuscript.

Place	Date	Hour	Summary of Events and Information	Remarks and references to Appendices
MONTIGNIES SUR-SAMBRE	Dec 18	7 pm	Moved from FONTAINE L'EVEQUE at 9 am along with 126 Inf Brigade. Left Brigade on line of March & proceeded to MONTIGNIES SUR SAMBRE. Brigade moved to GILLY. Personnel accomodated in Civilian Billets. [illegible]	
"	19	7 pm	Routine. Arranging beds for all personnel. Salved beds etc to fit up Hosp'l. Started Two 'Ablution' Sites one at MONTIGNY-S-SAMBRE for RFA 42D & another at GILLY for 126th Bde. [illegible]	
	20	7 pm	Routine. Lt Carroll RAMC rejoined the unit from No 5 C.C.S. [illegible]	
	21	7 pm	Lt Carroll detailed in Med. Charge of 42nd Machine-Gun Co. [illegible]	
	22	7 pm	Routine, [illegible]	
	23	7 pm	Routine. [illegible]	

A7092). Wt. W12839/M1293 750,000. 1/17. D. D & L., Ltd. Forms/C2118/14.

Instructions regarding War Diaries and Intelligence Summaries are contained in F. S. Regs., Part II. and the Staff Manual respectively. Title pages will be prepared in manuscript.

WAR DIARY
or
INTELLIGENCE SUMMARY.
(Erase heading not required.)

Army Form C. 2118.

Place	Date	Hour	Summary of Events and Information	Remarks and references to Appendices
MONTIGNIES SUR-SAMBRE	DEC 24th	7 pm	Routine. Cgw	
	25th	–	Routine. Xmas Dinner as usual for men with most of unit present. Lt Col Cunningham a/ADMS visited unit. Cgw	
	26th	–	Routine. Cgw	
	27th	–	Routine. Cgw	
	28th	–	Capt a/Lt Col H HENRY appointed to command of 1/2nd E. Lancs Fd Amb'ce to take effect from this date. Capt NEAME 1/2nd E Lancs Fd Amb posted for temp'y duty with 1/3rd E L Fd Amb Cgw. Appointed to & assumed command of unit. 8 patients admitted.	HH

A7092). Wt. W12839/M1293 750,000. 1/17. D. D & L., Ltd. Forms/C2118/14.

Army Form C. 2118.

Instructions regarding War Diaries and Intelligence Summaries are contained in F. S. Regs., Part II. and the Staff Manual respectively. Title pages will be prepared in manuscript.

WAR DIARY
or
~~INTELLIGENCE SUMMARY.~~

(Erase heading not required.)

Place	Date	Hour	Summary of Events and Information	Remarks and references to Appendices
MONTIGNIES SUR SAMBRE	29/12/18		Routine. Orders received from ADMS 42nd Divn to take Capt F.S. BEDALE M.C. on strength of this unit with effect from 25.12.18. Capt F.S. BEDALE had proceeded on leave to U.K. 11 patients admitted.	HH
"	30.12.18		Routine. Capt H. NEAME reported his return from temporary duty with 1/1 E. Lancs Field Amb. Capt A.M. GIBSON reported his departure to 1/3 E. Lancs Field Amb. in pursuance of orders issued by ADMS 42nd Div. 7 patients admitted.	HH
"	31.12.18		Routine. 5 patients admitted.	HH

Howard Henry
a/Lt Col RAMC(T)

Lieut. Col. R.A.M.C. (T.)
O.C. ½ East Lancs. Field Ambulance.

42 DIV

BOX 2475

WAR DIARY

OF

1/2nd EAST LANCASHIRE FIELD AMBULANCE

FROM :- January 1st, 1919 TO :- January 31st, 1919.

(VOLUME 1).

Jan 1919

Army Form C. 2118.

Instructions regarding War Diaries and Intelligence Summaries are contained in F. S. Regs., Part II. and the Staff Manual respectively. Title pages will be prepared in manuscript.

WAR DIARY
or
~~INTELLIGENCE SUMMARY.~~

(*Erase heading not required.*)

Place	Date	Hour	Summary of Events and Information	Remarks and references to Appendices
MONTIGNIES SUR SAMBRE	1.1.19		Field Ambulance H.Q at schools – RUE DES CARTIERES. Hospital accommodation good but limited in one portion of school. Good Dining Recreation + Lecture rooms for personnel. Satisfactory cookhouse accommodation and excellent QM stores. Stabling quite good but rather scattered in small stables holding 2 to 6 horses each. The following officers on strength of unit – Capt (a Lt Col) H. HENRY MC RAMC T.F. Commanding. Capt (a Maj) G A WEBSTER RAMC T.F. OC C Section. Capt F.S. BEDALE MC RAMC T.F. posted to unit after departure on leave to UK. Capt H NEAME RAMC T.C. Education & Demobilization officer. LIEUT P CARROLL RAMC T.C. on temporary duty with 42nd M.G.C. LIEUT + QM J LOWE Strength ORs RAMC 157 ASC H.T 30 ASC M.T 12 PB attached 2. Of whom following attached temporarily to other units 42nd Div Workshops 5 DHQ 3 42nd Div Reception Camp 1. 5 CCS 9. On leave U.K. 24. 43 horses on charge – being 2 deficient. Horsed vehicles complete. 4 Motor Ambulances in workshops + 2 Motor Cycles. 1 Bicycle deficient. The Ambulance is collecting sick from 126 Infy Bde Group located at ~~Gilly~~ GILLY – where there are 3 RAPs viz 1/5 E. Lancs Regt. 1/8 Manchester Regt 1/10 Manchester Regt + from RA Group located MONTIGNIES + CHATELINEAU 2 RAPs open. 211 Bde RFA + 42nd DAC. Sick Parade of 44 Labour Coy is being taken at F. Amb. H.Q. Two Early Treatment Centres for 'VD' are in operation one CHAUSSEE de FLEURUS. GILLY. + the other near Square MONTIGNIES. Horse Ambulances go out each morning to collect sick from Regimental Aid Posts. The Personnel are comfortably billetted in houses + the majority have beds. Educational classes are in progress. A fatigue party of 2 NCOs + 18 men working for RE. No parades to day except necessary fatigues. 7 patients admitted.	H.H.
" "	2.1.19		Routine. Fatigue party continues work for RE. 7 patients admitted	H.H.
" "	3.1.19		Routine Fatigue party to RE finishes today. 11 patients admitted	H.H.

A7092). Wt. W12839/M1293 750,000. 1/17. D. D & L., Ltd. Forms/C2118/14.

Instructions regarding War Diaries and Intelligence Summaries are contained in F. S. Regs., Part II. and the Staff Manual respectively. Title pages will be prepared in manuscript.

WAR DIARY

~~or~~

~~INTELLIGENCE SUMMARY.~~

(Erase heading not required.)

Army Form C. 2118.

Place	Date	Hour	Summary of Events and Information	Remarks and references to Appendices
MONTIGNIES-SUR-SAMBRE	4.1.19		Routine – 8 patients admitted	HH
" "	5.1.19		Routine 9 patients admitted	HH
" "	6.1.19		Routine. 12 OR + 4 GS wagons on fatigue at DRS with RE 6 patients admitted	HH
" "	7.1.19		Routine 12 OR + 2 GS wagons on fatigue at DRS with RE 8 patients admitted	HH
" "	8.1.19		Routine RE fatigue as yesterday. 60 visited RAP DAC + 210 Bde RFA. 6 patients admitted	HH
" "	9.1.19		Routine RE fatigue as yesterday. 60 visited RAP, 1/8 Manchester Regt + 1/10 Manchester Regt + 93rd Army RFA Bde. Early Treatment Centre opened at 42nd DAC RAP CHATELINEAU. 7 patients admitted	HH
" "	10.1.19		Routine Conference with Regimental Medical Officers re organization of medical supervision of units in GILLY + MONTIGNIES areas. Selected Central Medical Reception Room for GILLY at 31 CHAUSSEE de CHATELET. RE fatigue party 12 OR. 8 patients admitted	HH
" "	11.1.19		Routine. RE fatigue as yesterday. CAPT J. APPLEYARD RAMC 210 Bde RFA. Capt W H HEIR MBUSA 42nd DAC. 1st LIEUT J G STRICKLER MC USA 1/8 Manch. Regt. CAPT A L WHITE RAMC 1/10 Manch Regt attached to this unit for temporary duty. CAPT E R GREVILLE MC. RAMC 1/5 E. Lancs Regt (in UK on leave) also attached. RAMC orderly to AIDPOSTS of 1/5 E Lancs Regt 1/8 Manchester Regt. 1/10 Manchester Regt. 93rd Bd RFA. 210 Bde RFA + 42nd DAC. 3 patients admitted	HH
" "	12.1.19		Routine. Opened MEDICAL RECEPTION ROOM at GILLY. 3 patients admitted	HH
" "	13.1.19		Routine. Capt E R GREVILLE RAMC reported from leave to UK. Fatigue party 12 OR + 2 GS wagons to RE a/ADMS visited Medical Reception Room GILLY + expressed approval of plans. 8 patients admitted	HH
" "	14.1.19		Routine Fatigue party to RE as yesterday. 13 patients admitted	HH
"	15.1.19		LtCOL H Henry proceed for leave to UK and the command devolves on Major GA WEBSTER.	
	16.1.19		Routine 4 Patients admitted GAW	
	17.1.19		Routine 12 Patients admitted GAW	
	18.1.19		Routine 5 Patients admitted GAW	
	19.1.19		Routine 6 Patients admitted GAW	
	20.1.19		Routine 7 Patients admitted GAW	

A7092). Wt. W12839/M1293 750,000. 1/17. D. D & L., Ltd. Forms/C2118/14.

Army Form C. 2118.

WAR DIARY
or
INTELLIGENCE SUMMARY.
(*Erase heading not required.*)

Instructions regarding War Diaries and Intelligence Summaries are contained in F. S. Regs., Part II. and the Staff Manual respectively. Title pages will be prepared in manuscript.

Place	Date	Hour	Summary of Events and Information	Remarks and references to Appendices
MONTIGNIES SUR-SAMBRE	21.	7pm.	Routine 12 Patients admitted Capt	
" "	22	"	Routine 8 " " Capt	
" "	23	"	Routine 10 " " Capt	
" "	24	"	Routine 8 " " Capt	
" "	25	"	Routine 11 " " Capt	
" "	26	"	Routine 11 " " Capt	
" "	27	"	Routine 15 " " Capt	
" "	28	"	Routine 20 " " Major A M Gibson reported for duty, from 1/3 E Lancs Fd Amb taken on strength of Unit. Lt P. Carroll RAMC TC transferred 1/3. E Lancs Fd Amb and struck off strength of unit Capt	
" "	29.	"	Routine 16 Patients admitted Capt	
" "	30	"	Routine. 9 Patients admitted Lt Q.M JN LOWE promoted Capt Q.M. Capt	
" "	31	"	Routine. 5 Patients admitted, Capt	

C. Arthur [illegible]
Major RAMC T
1/2nd E. L. Fd Amb

A7092). Wt. W12839/M1293 750,000. 1/17. D. D & L., Ltd. Forms/C2118/14.

W A R D I A R Y.

1/2ND EAST LANCASHIRE FIELD AMBULANCE.

Vol.II

FEBRUARY 1 - 28th 1919.

Instructions regarding War Diaries and Intelligence Summaries are contained in F. S. Regs., Part II. and the Staff Manual respectively. Title pages will be prepared in manuscript.

WAR DIARY
or
~~INTELLIGENCE~~ SUMMARY.

(*Erase heading not required.*)

Army Form C. 2118.

Place	Date	Hour	Summary of Events and Information	Remarks and references to Appendices
MONTIGNIES S SAMBRE	1/2/19	7pm	Routine – 7 cases to MRS. CGS	
	2/2/19		Lt Col Henry M.C. O/C 1/2nd S.L. Fd Amb returned from leave in U.K. & assumed command of unit from this date. CGS	
			Routine 7 patients admitted HH.	
"	3.2.19		Routine 13 patients admitted HH.	
"	4.2.19		Routine. Attended conference at ADMS office re demobilization & formation of cadres. 13 patients admitted HH	
"	5.2.19		Routine Capt H NEAME RAMC TF proceeded for 14 days leave to UK. 8 patients admitted HH.	
"	6.2.19		Routine. 5 patients admitted HH.	
"	7.2.19		Routine. Cadre for unit selected. 5 patients admitted. HH	
"	8.2.19		Routine. 9 patients admitted HH.	
"	9.2.19		Routine Capt T S BEDALE MC RAMC TF struck off strength as from 25.1.19. 7 patients admitted	
"	10.2.19		Routine 12 patients admitted HH	
"	11.2.19		Routine 6 patients admitted HH. 8 class 'Y' horses sent to Base for U.K.	
"	12.2.19		Routine A/Major A M GIBSON proceeded for leave to UK. 5 patients admitted. HH	
"	13.2.19		Routine Capt A L WHITE RAMC(TF) reported his return from leave to UK. 5 patients admitted HH	
"	14.2.19		Routine 10 patients admitted HH	
"	15.2.19		Routine Capt & QM H M LOWE RAMC TF departed for leave to UK. 14 patients admitted HH	
"	16.2.19		Routine Capt A L WHITE RAMC(TF) proceeded to UK for Demobilization 12 patients admitted HH	
"	17.2.19		Routine 11 patients admitted HH.	

A7092). Wt. W12839/M1293 750,000. 1/17. D. D & L., Ltd. Forms/C2118/14.

Instructions regarding War Diaries and Intelligence Summaries are contained in F. S. Regs., Part II. and the Staff Manual respectively. Title pages will be prepared in manuscript.

WAR DIARY
or
~~INTELLIGENCE SUMMARY.~~
(Erase heading not required.)

Army Form C. 2118.

Place	Date	Hour	Summary of Events and Information	Remarks and references to Appendices
MONTIGNIES SUR SAMBRE	18.2.19		Routine 13 patients admitted HH	
"	19.2.19		Routine 12 patients admitted HH	
"	20.2.19		Routine 12 patients admitted HH	
"	21.2.19		Routine 6 patients admitted ~~HH~~ 4 Y class horses sent to base for sale HH	
"	22.2.19		Routine Capt H NEAME reported arrival from leave in UK. 11 patients admitted	HH
"	23.2.19		Routine 19 patients admitted HH	
"	24.2.19		Routine Capt H NEAME to assist in ADMS office vice DADMS. 1 patients admitted Mobilization Equipment not in use moved to room - Barracks Charleroi	HH
"	25.2.19		Routine 10 patients admitted HH	
"	26.2.19		Routine 8 patients admitted HH	
"	27.2.19		Routine 8 patients admitted 5 Y class horses sent to Base for sale HH	
"	28.2.19		Routine 4 patients admitted HH 21 ORs sent to concentration camp for demobilization during month HH	

Howard [illegible]
Lt Col

A7092). Wt. W12839/M1293 750,000. 1/17. D. D & L., Ltd. Forms/C2118/14.

www.ingramcontent.com/pod-product-compliance
Lightning Source LLC
Chambersburg PA
CBHW080854230426
43662CB00013B/2100